Rossi  Main Colliery

The Development of a Mining Community

Dave Fordham

Acknowledgements

The author would like to thank the following for their assistance in compiling this work: John Adam, Robert Astin, Brian Brownsword, Colin Dawson, Maureen Dossor, Norman Ellis, Richard Fordham, John Fordham, Paul Fox, Helen Hay, Roger Holmes, Mel Jones, Charles Kelham, John Petch, John Ryan, Richard Simons, Brian Tapson, Joan Ulley, Helen Wallder, and the staff of Doncaster Archives, Rotherham Archives and Sheffield Archives. Acknowledgment is also extended to Doncaster Local Studies Library for allowing access to contemporary newspaper records from *The Doncaster Gazette* and *The Doncaster Chronicle*, and to the staff of Doncaster Archives and the University of Birmingham Library for viewing their copies of The Colliery Guardian. Finally, I acknowledge a debt to the early postcard photographers whose work has been used to illustrate this publication - Edgar Scrivens and James Simonton & Sons. Every effort has been made to attribute copyright to the illustrations used in this publication. Unless otherwise credited, all illustrations featured in this publication are from the author's collection and all attempts to attribute copyright have been made.

Published by Fedj-el-Adoum Publishing
3 Adelaide Road, Norton, Doncaster, South Yorkshire, DN69EW
© Fedj-el-Adoum Publishing & Dave Fordham 2019

**Visit: www.fedjbooks.co.uk
for a list of our titles.**

ISBN 978-1-9161097-0-4

First Edition 2019

Printed in the UK

All rights reserved. No part of this publication may be reproduced, stored in a retrieval system, or transmitted, in any form or by any means, electronic, mechanical, photocopying, recording, or otherwise without written permission of the author.

Cover Illustration

A commercial postcard, published by James Simonton and Sons of Balby, showing shaft sinking operations at Rossington Colliery in 1914, with the No 2 shaft in the foreground. The small wooden building houses the temporary steam-powered winding engine used to raise and lower the kibbles in the shaft. The scaffolding to the left depicts the construction of one of the large winding engine houses built to accommodate the permanent winding engines.

Rossington Main Colliery

The Development of a Mining Community

Frontispiece: *This pen and ink study of Rossington Village by an unknown artist is one of a number illustrations that were published in the book 'Yorkshire Amalgamated Collieries: Modern Methods of Coal Production and Shipment' (c1928); a publication issued to celebrate the successful amalgamation of Denaby, Cadeby, Dinnington, Maltby and Rossington Collieries and promote the formation of Yorkshire Amalagamated Collieries. The illustration depicts newly completed housing provided by The Industrial Housing Association for colliery officials at the junction of Holmes Carr Road and West End Lane.*

Above: *A rather bored looking Mrs Deacon, resplendent in her hat and furs, is shown cutting the first sod for Rossington Colliery on 10 June 1912. The current location of the ceremonial silver spade is sadly unknown. The postcard was issued by Edgar Scrivens as part of a series of postcards of the ceremony.* (John Ryan Collection).

Part 1
Colour Illustrations

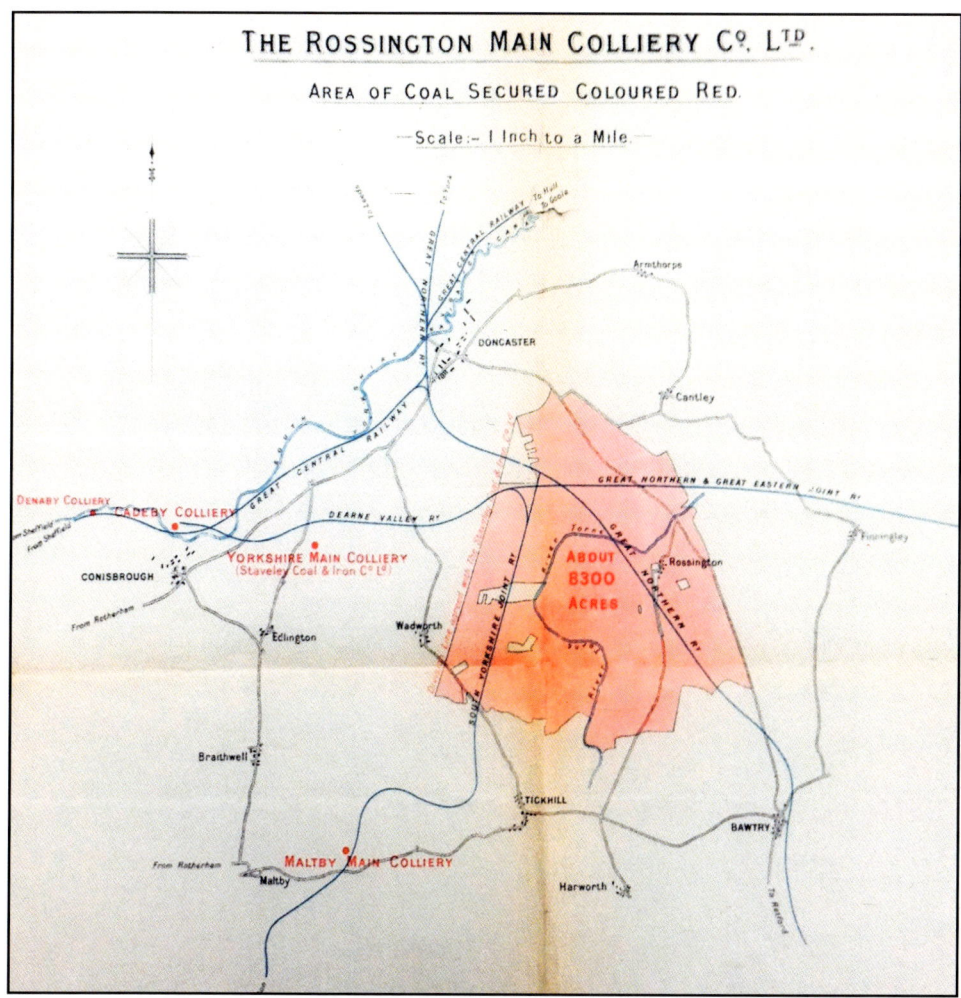

Above: *This plan was issued with the Rossington Main share prospectus and shows the royalty of 8,300 acres secured by the company, together with the surrounding railway lines. Over the following years, the royalty was increased to 9,000 acres. The issuing of shares to the public seems to have been largely unsuccessful as by 1927, 90% of the capital of the company had been taken by Sheepbridge and John Brown with only 10% held by outsiders.* (Reproduced with the consent of Rotherham Metropolitan Borough Council, Archives and Local Studies Service Reference 63-B/6/21/8).

Above: *Rossington Main Colliery captured on 30 August 1994 by Chris Allen. No 1 headgear is nearest the camera. Note the large chimney dating from c1914 - an unusal survivor when redevelopment work had occured at a pit. (© Chris Allen – www.geograph.org.uk/photo/177074)*

Below: *Rossington Main Colliery in 1998, viewed from the banks of the River Torne from the south with the partially grassed over spoil heap on the right. Most of the spoil heap was subsequently removed for road building purposes.*

Above: *A hand tinted postcard of Queen Mary's Road captured around 1921 as the Royal Hotel appears to be under construction. In this charming view, possibly the entire street has arranged itself for a group photograph!*

Below: *Another view from this series of hand tinted postcards published in the Vulcan Series by A Cooke of Rossington New Village. This view features the newly completed United Methodist Church on Nelson Road, prior to the completion of the extension to the building in 1928. The message on the back reads: "This is an old one of the chapel. They are building a nice new one next door. Laying foundation stone next Saturday".*

Above: *This shopping parade in King's Avenue was built by Frederick Hopkinson in 1915 and is shown here around 1920. The car, registered WR 405, would have been an unusual site at the time – did the vehicle belong to Doctor Kane or perhaps the Pit Manager?*

Below: *Holmes Carr Road – (here misspelt as Holmscar Road) formed part of a development of 147 houses built in 1926 by the Industrial Housing Association, mostly to house miners who had moved to Rossington from Northumberland and County Durham – hence this estate gained the nick name 'Geordieland'.*

Above: *Rossington Miners Welfare pictured from West End Lane. Prominent in the centre of the picture is the large ornate bandstand which was built in 1930.*

Below: *The reverse of another postcard of Rossington Miners Welfare showing a message written to Gwynedd Hudson of Brynteg near Wrexham. The writer, staying at 51 York Street, describes the pleasant nature of the area. Note the New Rossington postmark bearing the date of 11 September 1930.*

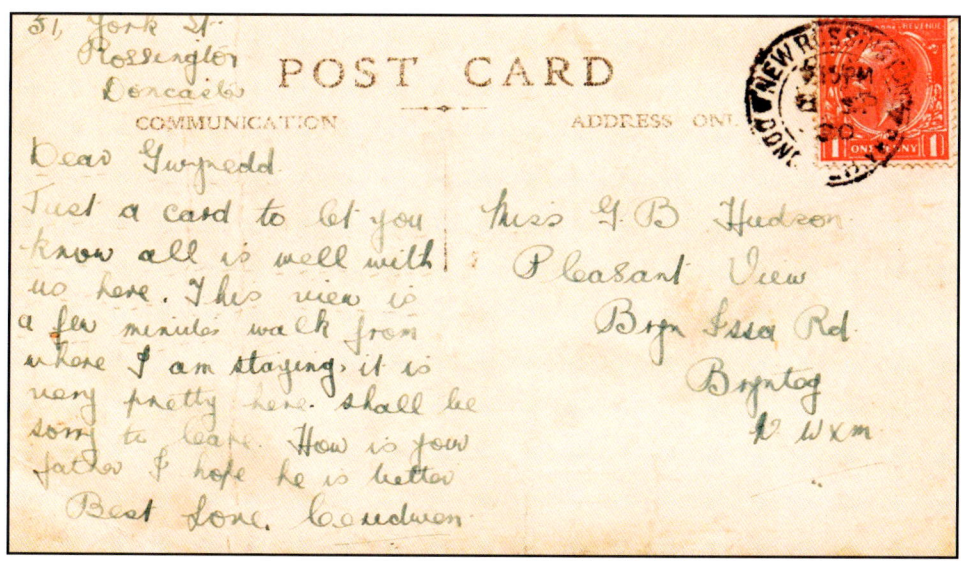

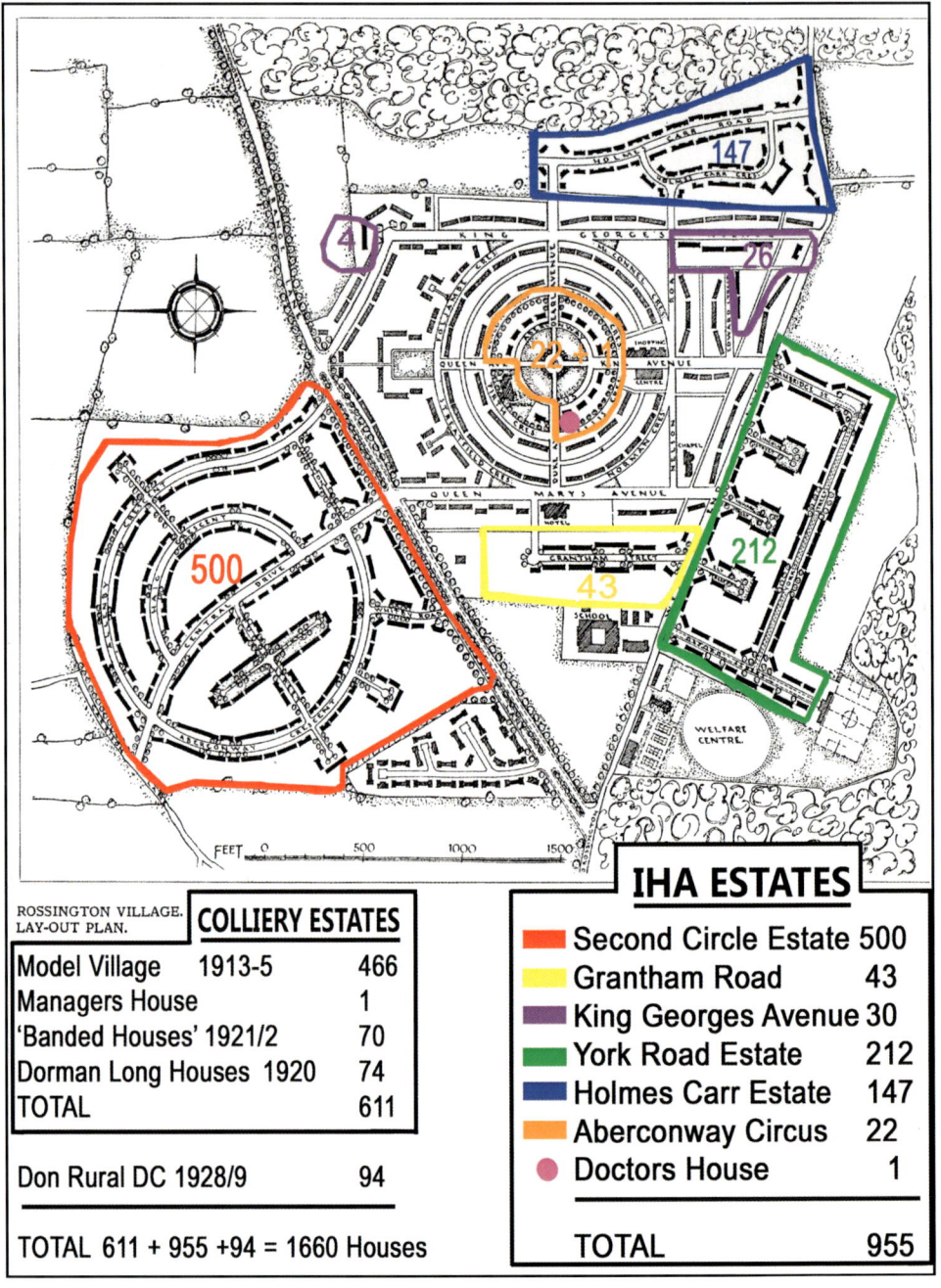

Below: *Linen plan for a block of four parlour cottages drawn up by Rossington Main Colliery in 1919 and submitted for approval by Maurice Deacon. These houses were built along the western side of King George's Road and were the first houses built following the suspending of building activities in 1916 due to the First World War. These commodious and attractively presented properties were some of the first in the country to adopt the design recommendations of the 1918 Tudor Walters Report, which had been commissioned by the Government. Sir John Tudor Walters would later design over 950 houses at New Rossington.* (Reproduced with the consent of DMBC Doncaster Archives – part of Heritage Doncaster, Reference RD/DON/P/332).

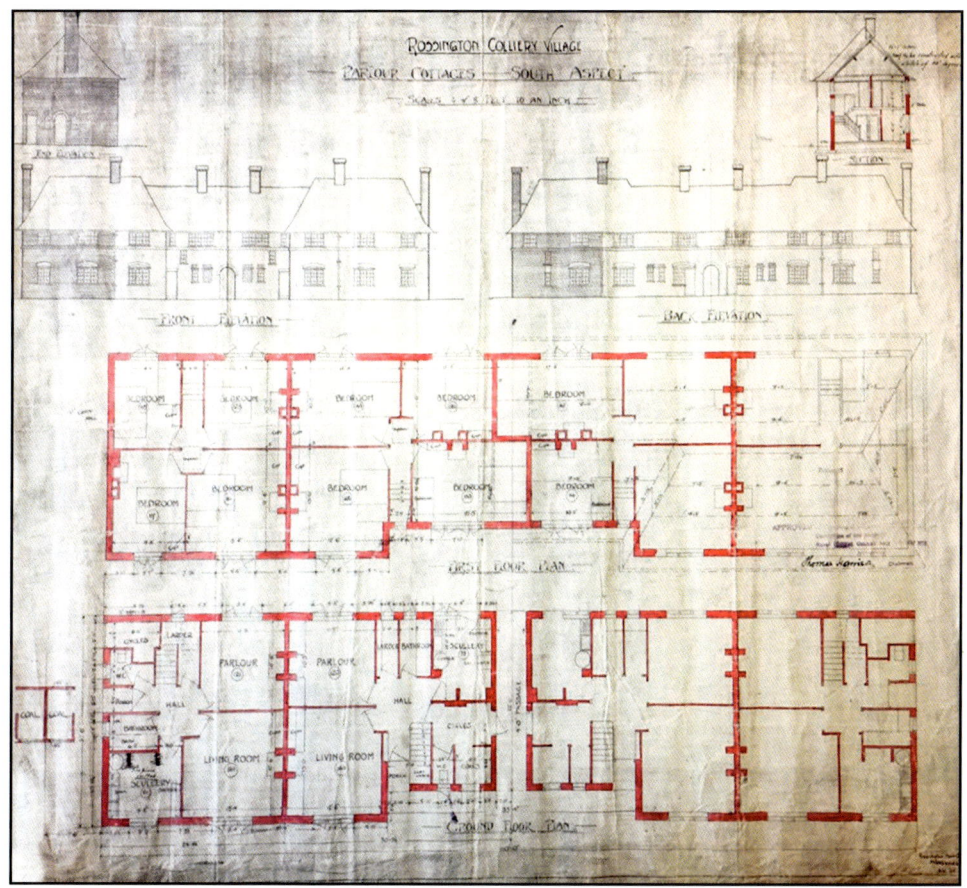

Opposite: *This plan of New Rossington was published in the book 'The Building of Twelve Thousand Houses' and shows the various blocks of houses (shaded black) built by the Industrial Housing Association* **(IHA)** *The six individual schemes are highlighted by the colour borders and the table on the lower left depicts the total number of houses built from 1913-1930 as calculated in this study. The 955 IHA houses at New Rossington was the greatest number of houses built by the IHA in any of the 35 different colliery villages that the association built throughout England and Wales.*

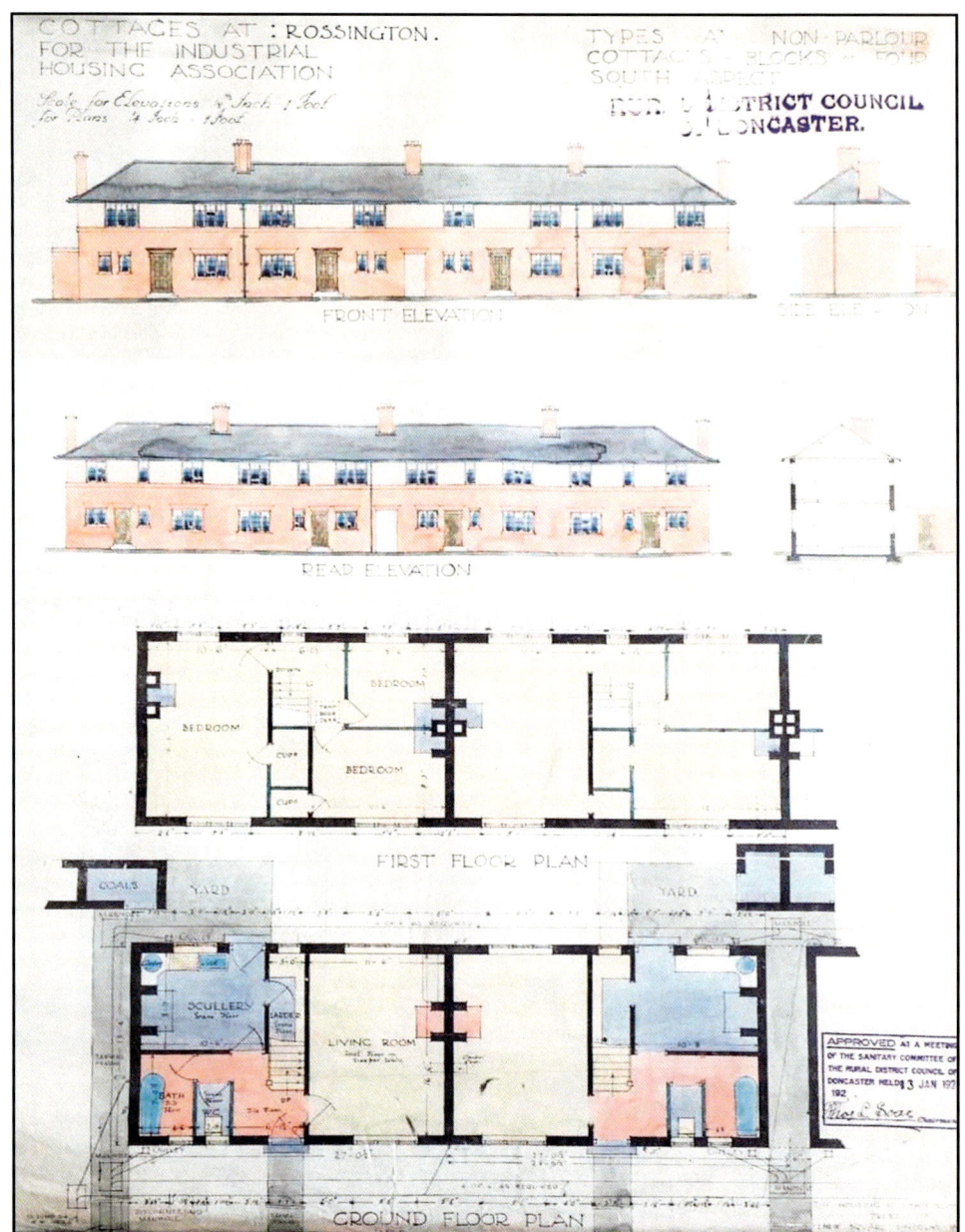

Above: *Plans drawn up by The Industrial Housing Association for Type A3 Non-Parlour cottages at Rossington. At the time is was common to refer to houses as 'parlour' (where they contained a living room and second sitting room or parlour) or non-parlour (where they featured a single larger living room). These houses were built on Grantham Road and in the York Road estate.* (Reproduced with the consent of DMBC Doncaster Archives – part of Heritage Doncaster, Refernce RD/DON/P/322).

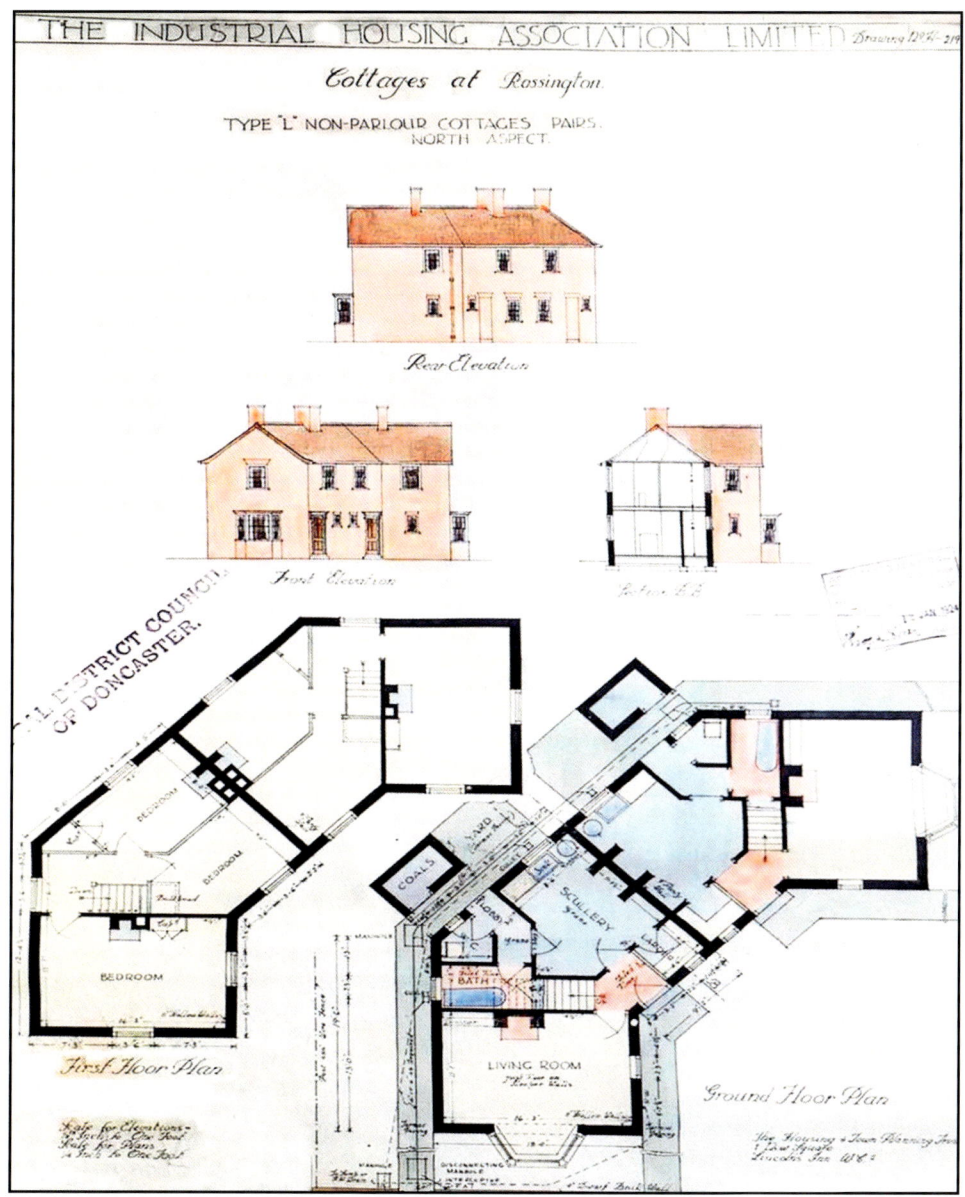

Above: *The Industrial Housing Association's Type L Non-Parlour Cottage was designed to form a corner feature at road junctions, and several of these were provided in the 'Second Circle Estate' on Grange Lane and on Central Drive. At the latter location, they were positioned around a cross roads – and enlarged into blocks of four. In reviewing the work of the Industrial Housing Association, Sir Patrick Abercrombie commended them for providing relatively expensive corner propertilike these. (Reproduced with the consent of DMBC Doncaster Archives – part of Heritage Doncaster, Reference RD/DON/P/322).*

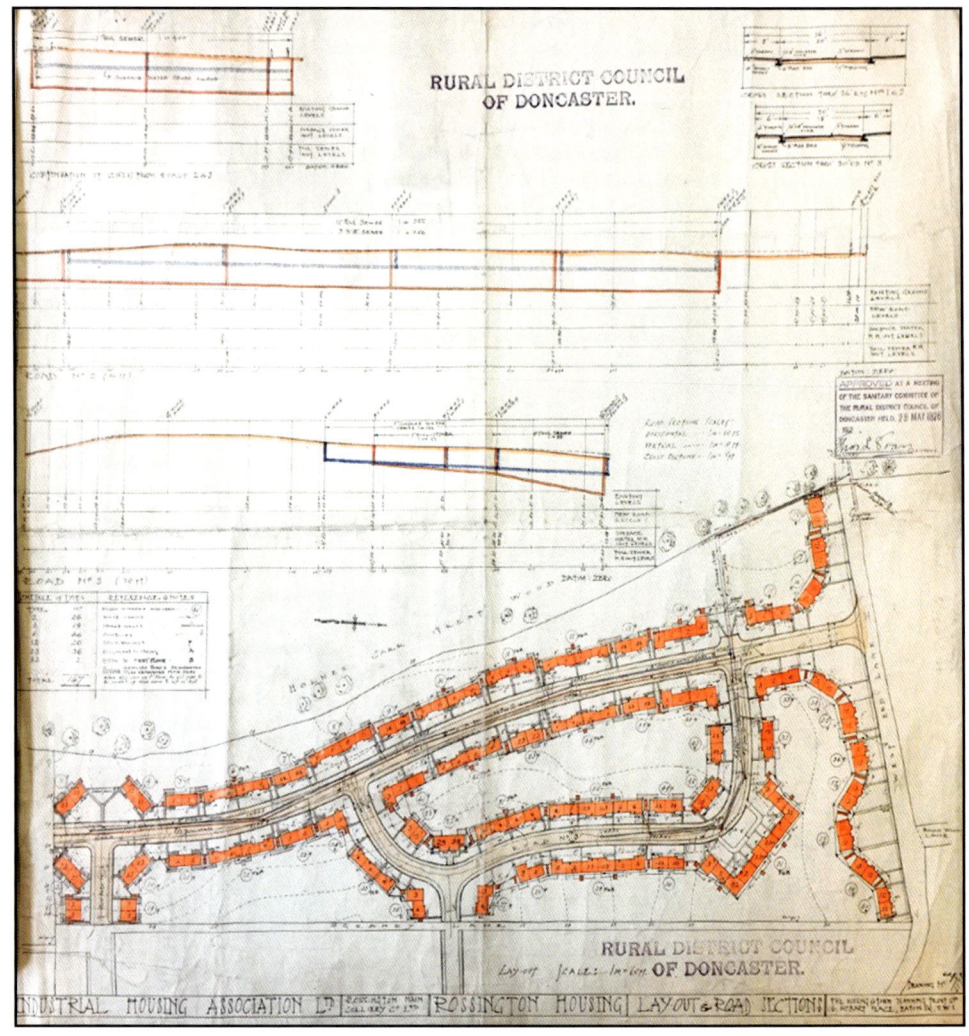

Above: *The last development by the Industrial Housing Association was the layout of 147 houses forming the Holmes Carr Estate and these plans were approved by the local authority on 29th May 1926. Larger houses in this development fronting West End Lane were built for pit deputies. The layout plan also features road gradients and the arrangement of a block of ten houses around a square on Holmes Carr Crescent. On completion, many families from the North-East moved to this area. The colliery company also located its works and estates department on Holmes Carr Road to oversee its portfolio of 1,570 houses.* (Reproduced with the consent of DMBC Doncaster Archives – part of Heritage Doncaster, Reference RD/DON/P/336*).*

Two views of Rossington's colourful buses from the lens of Richard Simons in the 1970s.

Above: *Blue Ensign JAK927N – a Roe bodied Daimler Fleetline - is about to make the turn into Duke Avenue from Queen Mary's Road. The Type 3 houses on the left form part of the First Circle Estate. The fleet number 1330 was applied to the vehicle following the purchase of the business by SYPTE in 1978, which helps to date the photograph*

Below: *A similar smartly presented Daimler Fleetline (registration MHE50P) belonging to Rossie Motors, arrives at the bus stop on Central Drive. The grey houses in the distance on Queen Mary's Road are steel framed Dorman Long houses which have since been demolished.*

Above: *Following the demolition of the colliery, Rossington Parish Council were able to arrange for the cast iron datestones from the two engine houses to be positioned in a small memorial garden at the junction of McConnell Crescent and King George's Road.*

Part 2
Rossington Main Colliery

Today, it is claimed by many that Rossington is the largest village in the country, yet, in the 1911 census, the population only numbered 371 inhabitants. The most recent census in 2011 recorded 13,557 people and the reason for this massive increase was the discovery of coal half a mile beneath the surface. This led to the development of Rossington Main Colliery in 1912 with its closure coming in 2006, after a life of nearly 100 years.

In the early 20th Century, prior to the coming of the colliery, Rossington was an estate village, with most of the population living in tenanted cottages and farms belonging to the Rossington Hall estate, a 3,166-acre estate owned by the local squire, Richard James Streatfeild*. Located around four miles to the south of Doncaster, on slightly elevated land above the flood plain of the River Torne just to the west of the Great North Road, the area consisted of several hamlets named Rossington, Littleworth, Rossington Bridge, Shooters Hill and Hesley. The settlement wasn't recorded in the Doomsday Survey of 1086, although the Romans had established a large fort at Rossington Bridge, an important staging point on the Roman Road from Doncaster to Lincoln. However, the name Rossington is believed to be of Anglo-Saxon derivation, meaning the 'farmstead on the moor'.

On the 4 September 1849, the Great Northern Railway opened a station to the west of Rossington on the main line from London to York. Despite this, the area still retained its rural character. Rossington village was centred around the church where the road from Tickhill joined the road to Doncaster and the lane to Rossington Station. This lane continued westwards beyond the level crossing as West End Lane with a track branching off as Grange Lane, passing Rossington Grange to link up with the village of Wadworth. Other facilities in Rossington at the time included an endowed national school, a vicarage, a post office, a small brickworks, an inn at Rossington Bridge, and an ornate wellhouse believed to be made from repurposed Roche Abbey stone.

* The original spelling of Streatfeild is shown here but this changed to Streatfield in the early 20th Century, an early reference being the naming of Streatfield Crescent on the proposed colliery village layout map of 1914. The modern spelling is used henceforth.

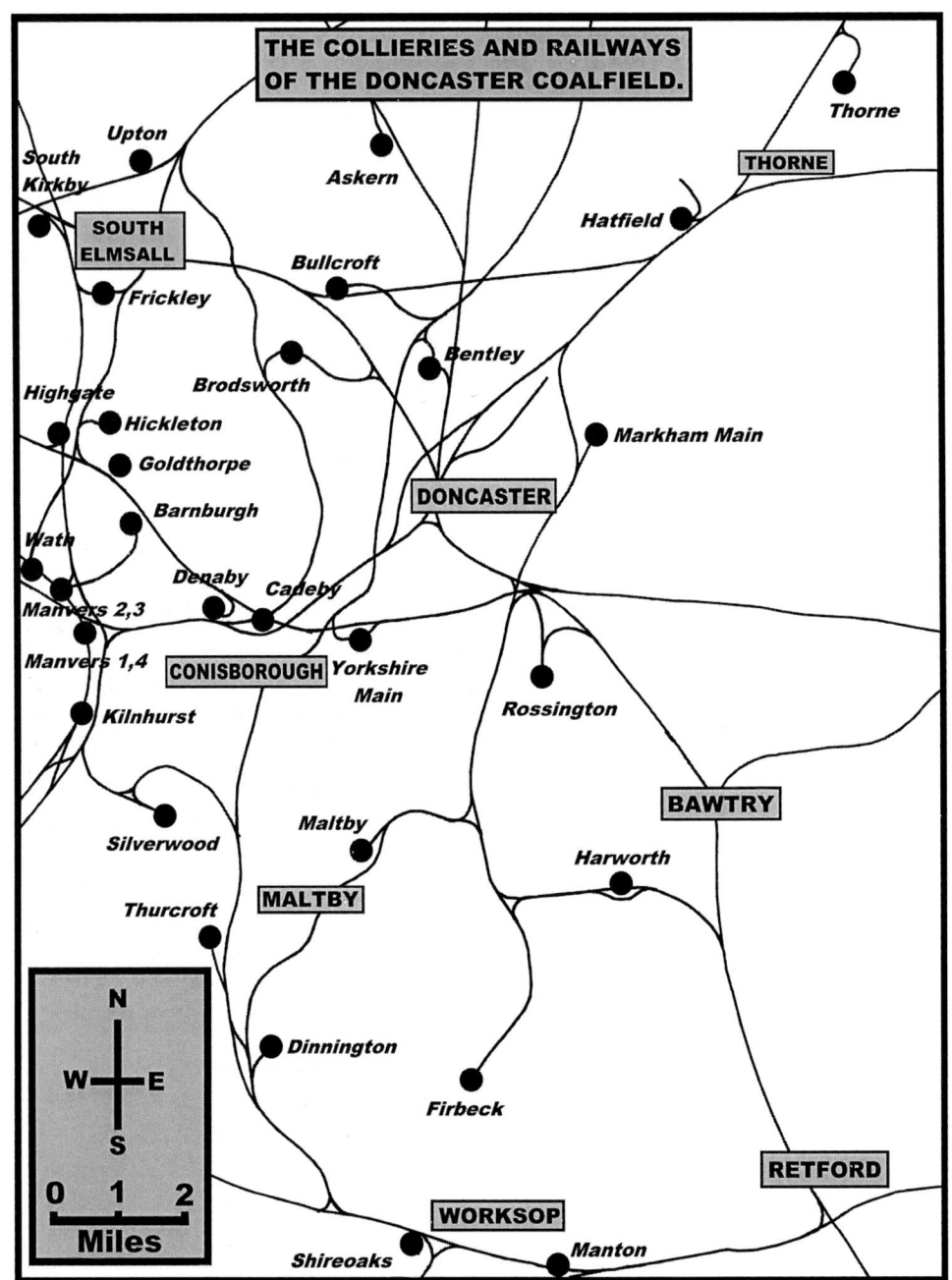

Above: *Map of the Doncaster area showing the locations of the various collieries with the railway network at its greatest extent, c1932. Rossington Main Colliery was located approximately four miles to the south of Doncaster.*

Above: *The manor of Rossington was originally owned by the Crown and was given by Henry VII to Doncaster Corporation. In 1771, Doncaster Corporation let the estate to their town clerk, James Stovin, who moved into a newly constructed mansion named Shooters Hill, around half a mile to the south of Rossington Church. In 1838, the estate was sold to James Brown, a woollen manufacturer from Leeds. Following his death in 1845, it was inherited by his son, James Brown Jr, and on his death in 1877 it passed to his nephew, Richard James Streatfield, who also had an estate at Uckfield in Sussex. Around 1880, Shooters Hill was destroyed by fire and a replacement house, named Rossington Hall was built in 1882 at a cost of £60,000. Richard Streatfield lived at Rossington Hall with his wife Mary and daughter Annette, until his death in 1931. Annette died six years later resulting in the estate being auctioned off in 1939, when many of the tenants purchased their cottages and farms. Rossington Hall was bought by The White Fathers, a Roman Catholic Order, and used as a missionary training college before being sold in 1948 to Doncaster Corporation. The Hall was then used as a special educational school by the local authority until its closure in 2008. After a few years of disuse, Gary and Michelle Gee purchased the property and have restored the mansion. The building is now used as a restaurant, wedding and conference centre. The postcard was published by Edgar Scrivens in 1910.*

In 1893, the Government sponsored a borehole at South Carr near Haxey, around eight miles to the east of Rossington. This borehole proved the existence of several coal seams including the famous 'Barnsley Seam' at a depth of 1,067 yards. The coal seams are all contained within rocks known as the Coal Measures which belong to the Carboniferous geological era. The borehole had confirmed the eastwards extension of the Coal Measures strata (from their outcrop in the Barnsley and Rotherham areas where they are exposed at the surface – hence the naming of the Barnsley Seam) into the Doncaster area, concealed beneath a cover of much younger Permian limestones and Triassic sandstones. The Doncaster Coalfield was hence known as a 'concealed coalfield' as the coal seams are not visible at the surface.

Two charming photographs captured by Matthew Henry Stiles featuring rural village life in Rossington in the late 19th Century.

Above: *The 14th century St Michael's Church was largely rebuilt in 1844 (although the original tower was retained) at the expense of James Brown, the owner of the Rossington estate at the time.*

Below: *Fountain Cottages were very smartly presented estate cottages built in an Elizabethan style. The railway employee appears to have unofficially appropriated a Great Northern Railway sack barrow to give a ride to the young boy. The unusual building beyond Fountain Cottages was the Ivy House Farm slaughterhouse.*

Above: *The other major land owner in the Rossington area was Benjamin Ingham Whitaker of Hesley Hall whose estate included land straddling the former Yorkshire / Nottinghamshire border. Benjamin Whitaker was the eldest of 12 children, all born at Palermo in Italy, and he was formerly a Lieutenant in the West Yorkshire Yeomanry Cavalry and High Sherriff of Nottinghamshire. He died in 1922 and his wife continued to live at Hesley until 1941 when Sir Albert Whitaker inherited the Hesley estate. The hall was subsequentlyused by the Central Council for the Care of Cripples, and in 1975 it was acquired by The Hesley Group, who continue to run the property as a school for adults and young people with learning difficulties. The postcard view above was issued by Edgar Scrivens in 1910.*

At the start of the 20th Century, the global demand for coal was increasing by 4% per year and the UK was the world's leading exporter of coal. Between 1896 and 1904, the total profits from coal mining in the country had quadrupled; thus, the financial incentives for new colliery developments were certainly attractive. As well as the export trade, domestic consumption was increasing as the country was reliant upon coal to fuel the furnaces of industry, the railway and shipping networks and the growing domestic use by a rapidly increasing population. During the Victorian and Edwardian era, the British Empire had become a booming steam-powered economy fuelled by coal. Industrialists were keen to exploit the nation's coal reserves, and great riches lay waiting in the concealed coalfield surrounding Doncaster for investors with the appropriate financial muscle and engineering expertise. During the first decade of the 20th Century, plans were made to carve up the countryside around Doncaster into a series of regions of 10-15 square miles each, known as 'royalties'. The intention was to sink a pit at the centre of each royalty, thus surrounding the town with a circle of large collieries.

Above: *Rossington Railway Station opened on 4th September 1849 and passenger facilities closed on 6th October 1958 before the station closed completely on 7th December 1964. This postcard view published by James Simonton in the 1930s shows the the level crossing on West End Lane looking into Old Rossington with Gattison Grange in the distance. For many years, this road was the only entrance to and from New Rossington, and the delays caused by the crossing gates were a frequent inconvenience to the local community.*

Concurrently with the move to develop the large collieries around Doncaster by the industrial concerns of the day, was the urge by the landed gentry to encourage such developments, as coal royalties could provide an extensive addition to estate incomes. For landowners like Richard Streatfield of Rossington Hall, traditional estate receipts from agriculture, woodland, tied farms and cottages, would be potentially dwarfed by the income from coal royalties. Therefore, it was in the landowner's interests to negotiate leases with colliery speculators who would be liable for annual rents and a royalty on every ton of coal produced once a coal mine came into production.

However, with coal lying at such depth in the concealed coalfield around Doncaster, it would require the latest technological advances in mining engineering to enable the successful exploitation of these reserves. For a profit to be generated, each of the Doncaster pits would have to command a huge royalty of up to 10,000 acres and employ a workforce of around 3,000 men with the aim of producing 1,000,000 tons of coal per year, all of this set in a rural background with no pre-existing railway connections and very little by the way of a local workforce. This in turn resulted in the need to construct a new settlement to house the colliery personnel, together with various shops, schools, churches, pubs etc, to service this new population.

In 1898, Dalton Main Collieries Ltd. was formed with a capital of £200,000, to acquire the small Roundwood Colliery near Rotherham and establish a large pit at Silverwood, near Thrybergh - around 10 miles to the west of Rossington. The sinking of Silverwood Colliery commenced in April 1900 and the Barnsley Seam was encountered in December 1903 at a depth of 746 yards. Silverwood colliery was an immediate success and by 1910 the pit claimed to be the largest in the Yorkshire Coalfield, employing a workforce of 3,228 and generating substantial profits from an output of over 1,000,000 tons per year.

Buoyed by the success of Silverwood Colliery, Dalton Main Collieries began to look to the east of the Silverwood royalty to acquire coal leases beneath the estates of other landowners. Negotiations were quickly opened with the Countess of Yarborough at Conisbrough and Earl Fitzwilliam, owner of Edlington Woods. However, in 1907, the Dalton Main Colliery came into conflict with a rival colliery owner, the Staveley Coal & Iron Company of Chesterfield, who were negotiating with several landowners in the Edlington, Warmsworth and Balby areas. At a board meeting that year, the Dalton directors decided to focus on obtaining coal royalties in the Rossington and Braithwell areas, thus surrounding the Staveley company on three sides and preventing any further expansion by the rival concern. With this in place, the Dalton directors hoped that an arrangement could be made with their neighbours, including the potential to jointly share the new coalfields, rather than engaging in a competition for mineral rights.

Subsequently, Dalton Main Collieries negotiated eight coal leases to form what they termed The Rossington Coalfield:

Lease 1. Richard James Streatfield of Rossington Hall. Signed 19th August 1909 for a period of 60 years from 1st January 1908 (3,166 acres). Colliery to be situated on Streatfield land at Holmes Carr Pastures.

Lease 2. John Jarratt of Elmfield House, Doncaster, owner of the Bessecarr Manor estate. Signed 30th March 1910 for a period of 75 years from 1st July 1909 (144 acres).

Lease 3. George Savile Foljambe of Osberton Hall, Worksop, owner of agricultural land in Wadworth, Stancil and Tickhill. Signed 27th April 1910 for a period of 80 years from 1st January 1910 (2,500 acres).

Lease 4. Benjamin Ingham Whitaker of Hesley Hall. Signed 27th April 1910 for a period of 58 years from 1st January 1910 – (acreage not given).

Lease 5. Frank Parker-Rhodes, Rotherham Solicitor. Acting on behalf of John Lionel Wordsworth owner of surface lands in Wadworth and Wellingley. Signed 30th May 1911 – (acreage and effective date not given).

Lease 6. John Jarratt of Elmfield Hall, Doncaster, owner of the Wellingley estate and Stancil Farm. Signed 21st July 1911 for a period of 80 years from 1st January 1906 - (acreage and effective date not given).

Lease 7. Staveley Coal & Iron Company – sublease from Elizabeth Catherine Banks of St Catherine's Hall, Balby. Signed 20th July 1911 for a period of 80 years from 1st January 1906 – (acreage not given).

Lease 8. Staveley Coal & Iron Company – sublease from Sophia Flora Skipwith of Loversall Hall. Signed 24th July 1911 for a period of 80 years from 1st January 1906 (100 acres).

The total royalty of all eight leases secured 8,300 acres. As can be seen from the particulars of leases 7 and 8, the Dalton and Staveley Companies had come to an arrangement in the meantime, with Dalton gaining coal in the Balby and Loversall areas that could be more easily worked from the new pit at Rossington, whilst they conceded land in Conisbrough belonging to the Countess of Yarborough which could be more easily worked from Staveley's new Edlington Colliery. This process was known as negotiating boundary lines between neighbouring pits in order to facilitate workings, and also served to stop unofficial poaching of coal belonging to a neighbouring colliery!

The intricate negotiation of coal leases and royalties usually involved much to-ing and fro-ing between landowners, agents to the estates, solicitors and the colliery companies, and this could subsequently lead to delays in putting a coal royalty together. Coal leases were complex legal documents and subject to various clauses to protect the interests of both parties. As an example, the Rossington Hall lease contains the following clause:

"Excepting and reserving to the leaser all game, woodcock, snipes, landrails, wild fowl, rabbits and fish with the exclusive right for him and all persons authorised by him at all times of preserving the same and of hunting shooting, fishing, coursing and sporting over and on any of the colliery surface lands".

The lease documents also contain the royalties due to be paid and Lease 6 gives a typical example:

> *"Royalty of £25 per foot thickness per acre for the first 12 years following the shafts striking the Barnsley seam, followed by a royalty of £27/10s per foot thickness per acre from Year 13 onwards until the end of the lease period."*

With the Barnsley seam expected to be 6 feet thick, this would equate to 6 x £25 for every acre of coal, which typically works out at six pence per ton. In addition, an annual rent was due for each royalty owner, which usually increased during the period of the lease. Richard Streatfield would also receive another payment known as wayleave - as coal beneath the estates of the neighbouring seven land owners would have to be brought to the surface at a pit which had been sunk on his land.

As the coal leases were being negotiated with the various landowners, the success of Dalton Main Collieries Ltd with Silverwood Colliery had attracted the attention of an even larger industrial conglomerate named John Brown & Company Ltd of Sheffield. John Brown owned several pits in the Rotherham area at Aldwarke, Carr House and Canklow, together with their steelworks at Atlas near Sheffield. They also had extensive ship building interests on the River Clyde at Glasgow. In 1909, John Brown purchased a controlling interest in Dalton Main Collieries Ltd, with the aim of developing the Rossington Coalfield which, in addition to supplying the profitable London markets and export trade, would also be a cheap source of coal for their shipping and steel interests.

The Chairman of John Brown was Lord Aberconway of Bodnant. Born as Charles Bright Benjamin McLaren in 1850, he served as Liberal MP for the Stafford constituency from 1880-1886 and for the Bosworth constituency from 1892-1910. However, despite his political career, he became increasingly involved with the management of various industrial companies following the death of his father in law, Henry Davis Pochin. From 1864 onwards, Henry Pochin and his business partner David Chadwick had established 47 limited liability companies with interests in chemicals, china clay, coal and steel - and one of these companies was the Sheffield steelmaker John Brown who inherited the Rossington leases.

However, recognising the potential expense and difficulty in developing the Rossington royalty, on 25 July 1910, John Brown and Lord Aberconway approached another colliery company with the proposal of forming a joint venture. This company was the Sheepbridge Coal & Iron Company of Chesterfield, one of the 47 limited liability companies established by Henry Pochin and, where Lord Aberconway also conveniently served as a director - subsequently being promoted to Chairman of Sheepbridge.

Sheepbridge Coal & Iron Company operated iron and steel works at Chesterfield and owned pits at Glapwell and Langwith in Derbyshire. In 1902, they had successfully joined with the Sheffield Coal Company to develop Dinnington Main Colliery and in 1904 they were actively securing various leases which would form the Maltby Coalfield which adjoined the Rossington Coalfield to the south west. When the shafts of Maltby Main Colliery struck coal in 1910, this caused the proposed Rossington venture to look very enticing and consequently Sheepbridge accepted the invitation to join John Brown in developing Rossington Colliery.

On 15th July 1911, the Rossington Main Colliery Company Ltd (company number 116,849) was registered with a capital of £500,000 in order to acquire the eight leases secured by Dalton Main Collieries and develop the Rossington pit.

The first directors (who would be paid £1,200 per year for their services), were:

Charles McLaren, Lord Aberconway (Chairman)
Maurice Deacon (Managing Director)
Charles Ellis, Bernard Firth, Frederick Fowler, W H McConnel & Walter McLaren MP

In addition, Mr T E Haslam was appointed as Secretary, Mr A Thompson was appointed as Agent and Coningsby Phillips was recruited from Wath Main Colliery and appointed as the first colliery manager.

Of the above directors, Maurice Deacon, Frederick Fowler, W H McConnel and Walter McLaren were directors of Sheepbridge, and Charles Ellis and Bernard Firth were directors of John Brown. Walter McLaren was Lord Aberconway's younger brother. The new company would have its registered office at the Sheepbridge Works in Chesterfield and have a capital of £500,000 which was considered enough to develop the pit and a colliery village of 1,000 houses. The capital was divided into 500,000 £1 shares of which Sheepbridge subscribed for 255,000 shares giving them a controlling majority, and John Brown subscribed for 120,000 shares. The remaining 125,000 shares would be offered to the public and a prospectus was published inviting investors to purchase shares in return for a potential annual dividend paid to shareholders from profits from the new company. Judging from estimates from the depth of coal at nearby Maltby Colliery, they expected to find coal at Rossington at a depth of 850-900 yards and it was hoped that the Barnsley seam would have a thickness of around 6-7 feet. The directors had such confidence that coal would be struck, that they dismissed the need for any exploratory boreholes. It was proposed to sink a large pit and build surface equipment to deal with an output of 5,000-6,000 tons of coal per day which would enable the pit to produce 1,000,000 tons of coal per year for a period of 80 years. As part of the arrangement, the new company would purchase the eight coal leases from Dalton Main Collieries for £1,159 and pay them an additional fee of a penny for every ton of coal produced at Rossington Main Colliery.

With the funding in place, the Rossington Main Colliery Company began preparations for sinking the new pit. A site of 105 acres was selected in fields to the west of Holmes Carr Wood near the River Torne and over a mile from Rossington Church. The proposed colliery village would be positioned on an 85-acre site to the east of Holmes Carr Wood and thus the pit would not be visible from the village. Negotiations were commenced with the Great Northern Railway to build a temporary branch line in order to access the new pit. This would also enable materials and plant to be delivered to the site and once the pit was operational, the temporary branch line could be replaced with a permanent railway connection. In 1911, the Great Northern Railway received parliamentary approval to construct the branch line.

At the end of 1911, materials were delivered to the site and it was expected to employ a team of 200-300 sinkers to undertake the difficult and dangerous work of sinking the two shafts to the Barnsley seam, which could take up to three years. The sinkers had just completed the successful sinking of the shafts of Maltby Main Colliery and they transferred en masse to Rossington - complete with several large wooden huts with corrugated iron roofs that served as accommodation blocks and mess halls. They also brought over their own wooden school for their children which had been provided by the West Riding County Council when they were at Maltby. The temporary settlements formed by the sinker's huts were situated on West End Lane near Holmes Carr Wood. Such settlements were variously known as 'Tin Towns'.

On Monday 10th June 1912, a special train left Doncaster Railway Station and travelled to Rossington Railway Station from which it accessed the temporary branch line to the colliery site. The train carried a compliment of colliery directors and invited guests to a special ceremony for the 'cutting of the first sod'. Amongst the guests were the colliery directors, the local landowners, the Doncaster and Rossington vicars, representatives from the local councils and authorities, railway company officials and various other attendees, including as the *Doncaster Gazette* reporter noted – members of the fairer sex!

In front of a wooden stage and beneath a large steam-powered crane from which the Union Jack fluttered in the breeze, Lord Aberconway chaired the proceedings. He presented Mrs Maurice Deacon with a handsome ceremonial silver spade and invited her to cut the first sod of turf above the site of No 1 Shaft. So vigorously did Mrs Deacon perform this duty, that she managed to buckle the silver blade in the soil. Nevertheless, she reversed the spade and flattened the blade with her foot and continued digging. Lord Aberconway thanked Mrs Deacon for performing the ceremony and joked that it was evident that the soil wanted a good deal of turning!

Lord Aberconway then performed the cutting of the first sod above the site of Number 2 shaft before the party adjourned to one of the wooden huts where a luncheon was provided, and numerous speeches and toasts were made. Lord Aberconway spoke of the proposed Rossington Colliery village and its future inhabitants:

Above: *Local photographer Edgar Leonard Scrivens was invited to the "Cutting the First Sod" ceremony to record the event and the photographs were reproduced in contemporary newspaper reports and issued as a set of six postcards. Number 1 in this set details the assembled throng of guests, complete with several children.*

> "...they hoped to build a mining village giving their men the best conditions that modern science demanded, together with all those advantages that the working man was entitled to....with institutes, churches and chapels, good schools, and in a pleasant country district, they ought to attract the best type of collier that the country could produce anywhere and with the best type of collier they might consider that the future was ensured".

Once the ceremony had been completed, the actual work of sinking the shafts could commence. Some of the permanent surface buildings had already been constructed, and steel headgears were built above each shaft. Two small temporary winding engines would be attached to each shaft and these would be used for sinking operations. Once coal was found, permanent steam-powered winding engines would be installed and two such engines were ordered from Markham & Company, a manufacturer of steam engines. These engines would be housed in two large engine houses which would be connected by a power house. Steam production would be provided by five Lancashire boilers and exhaust steam and smoke would be vented through a large chimney.

The team of shaft sinkers commenced the work of sinking a pair of shafts. The No 1 shaft would be 22 feet in diameter whilst the No 2 shaft would have a smaller diameter of 20 feet. Several other shaft sinkings at pits in the Doncaster area had been plagued by water seeping from the younger limestones and sandstones that overlay the Coal Measures rocks, and, in anticipation of this, pumps were provided. The sinkers worked 20 to each shaft, in a three-shift system per day, seven days a week. They used compressed air drills to excavate the stone which was loaded by hand into a large iron bucket known as a kibble. The kibble was then raised up the shaft and its excavated material discarded. The kibble was also the way in which the sinkers travelled to the bottom of their shafts at the start and end of their shifts. As the shafts were deepened, the walls were lined with 9-inch brickwork and iron tubbing forming a circular collar- and the voids between the brick wall and the surrounding rock were filled with cement grouting to form a waterproof boundary.

Slow progress was made through the water bearing strata and after 9 months of work, No 1 shaft was only 48 yards deep and No 2 shaft had only reached a depth of 30 yards. In the meantime, the colliery company continued to develop the surface plant including the coal screens and railway sidings and commenced building the new village. By March 1914, the No 1 shaft had reached a depth of 275 yards and No 2 shaft 172 yards. The slow progress was attributed to pumping out water. However, once the Coal Measures rocks were encountered, operations were expected to proceed at a faster rate, without any serious interruptions.

Above: *Another illustration from Edgar Scriven's 'Cutting the First Sod' series of postcards shows the assembled dignitaries inspecting the large iron bucket known as the kibble suspended from the jib of the steam powered crane. This kibble would be attached to the headgear and used to lower the sinkers down the shafts at the start of each shift and would typically hold around six men – today's Health & Safety Officers would have a fit!*

Below: *Mrs Deacon is pictured in the centre, whilst Lord Aberconway carries the ceremonial silver spade at the Rossington Main 'Cutting the First Sod' ceremony on 10th June 1912.*

Above: *Shaft sinking was notoriously wet work, and the sinkers dressed in oil skins and sou'westers as if they were fisherman going to sea. Their work was relatively well paid but extremely dangerous and several shaft sinkers lost their lives whilst performing this duty at other pits. Fortunately, the Rossington shafts were serious accident free. This team of sinkers, pictured above at No 2 shaft, had sunk Dinnington, Maltby and Rossington collieries and, once their work was completed, many of them moved onwards to sink the shafts at Firbeck Main Colliery, although some stayed to work at Rossington. Three of the sinkers have been identified: on the back row, far right, is Peter Wedd; third from right is Jack Harley; on the front row, second from the left, is George Hearne.*

During 1914, the colliery company spent £96,377 on developing the pit, a total expenditure since 1911 of £267,456. Sinking operations continued and the directors were somewhat relieved when on 4th May 1915, the No 1 shaft intercepted the Barnsley Seam at a depth of 872 yards. The seam was found to be 6 feet and 7 inches thick and of good quality. To celebrate, the Union Jack was flown from the headgears. At the time, the No 2 shaft had reached a depth of 600 yards and it was decided to continue deepening both shafts to intercept a secondary seam called the Dunsil Coal Seam. On 14th May 1915, No 1 shaft reached the Dunsil Seam at a depth of 888; it was found to be 5 feet and 6 inches in thickness.

On 7th November 1915, No 2 shaft finally intercepted the Barnsley Seam, and this shaft was deepened to reach the Dunsil Seam on 18th November 1915. Both shafts were deepened to a sump at a depth of 895 yards. It was proposed to load coal into the shafts at the Dunsil horizon, but work the Barnsley Seam first, and this would be accessed by inclined drifts from the Dunsil level. With two thick coal seams found in close proximity, Lord Aberconway announced that *"Rossington pit will be one of the most profitable in the South Yorkshire Coalfield"*.

Above: *Regina Press Photographers were also at the Cutting the First Sod ceremony to record a series of photographs which featured in the Doncaster Gazette published on Friday 12 June 1912. The captions to the photographs are reproduced here:* **CUTTING THE FIRST SOD OF THE NEW COLLIERY** *(1) General view of the sod cutting proceeding. (2) Mrs Maurice Deacon cutting the first sod. (3) Right to Left – Mr Maurice Deacon (Managing Director), Mrs Deacon, Miss Deacon, Mr B A Firth (Sheffield), Mrs Firth, Mr A Thompson (agent, Rossington), Mr C W Phillips (manager, Rossington). (4) Lord Aberconway (Chairman of Messrs John Brown and Co, Sheffield). (5) Special G N train conveying guests to and from the ceremony.*

Opposite: A *splendid view of No 2 shaft recorded by James Simonton in 1914. This postcard features sinking operations at the shaft using the permanent steel lattice headgear. Within this structure can be seen a pulley wheel around which a rope is wound around from the shaft to the temporary winding engine housed in the wooden structure on the left.*

453. Rossington Colliery. No 2 Shaft J.S.&S.

During 1916, with their work at Rossington completed, most of the 300 sinkers and their families moved to their next project, sinking the shafts at Firbeck Colliery, another pit in which the Sheepbridge Company had an interest. At Rossington the two shafts were both able to wind coal and equipped with triple deck cages, each able to carry 9 tubs of coal with each draw. With 466 houses now completed in the colliery village, the pit was ready to extract coal and that year 107,800 tons were produced, mostly from the construction of tunnels and roadways through the shaft pillar and roadways into the Barnsley Seam in order to open several advancing longwall coal faces. Recruitment campaigns were carried out and men and their families, mostly from the older mining regions of Yorkshire, Lancashire, Derbyshire, Nottinghamshire, Durham and Wales moved into the new village to start a life at Rossington Main Colliery.

During 1917, a permanent steam-powered ventilation fan was installed on the surface by the Waddle Engineering & Fan Company. This drew air down the No 1 downcast shaft and through the underground workings, with foul air being expelled via the No 2 upcast shaft, thus keeping the workings freshly ventilated. With the ventilation system established, full production commenced at the pit with a workforce of 783 men. The men worked an 8-hour shift system, day shifts starting at 6am, after shifts from 2pm and night shifts from 10 pm. Coal cutting was undertaken on the days and afters shift only, men on the night shift being employed on safety work and undertaking preparation for coal cutting by the following shift. The men were allowed a 20-minute snap break during the shift for the consumption of their sandwiches, usually bread and jam or bread and dripping and contained within a metal snap tin with liquid refreshment (usually water or weak tea) contained in a large metal containers called a Dudley. Smoking was strictly prohibited on account of the threat of gas, so many men had a tin of snuff or a pouch of chewing tobacco.

Coal was won from a series of advancing longwall faces in the Barnsley Seam, divided into tub stalls. Once established, the advancing longwall face was an efficient method of coal working. Miners would undercut the coal along the width of the coal face, removing coal as it fell, and using wooden pit props to control the fall of the roof behind the face. As work advanced into the coalface, the pit props were removed allowing the overlying rock to naturally collapse into the void created known as the 'gob', whilst maintaining a safe working space along the coalface. Teams of 8 colliers worked along the coal face and loaded the coal by hand into tubs which could hold 15 cwt of coal. These were then hauled by pit pony to the main roadway from which an endless rope haulage driven by compressed air delivered the tubs to the pit bottom for raising to the surface.

On the surface, the tubs of coal travelled down a gravity-driven incline to the screens building, a noisy and dusty building containing various tumblers, rotary screens, oscillating screens and conveyor belts - all powered by steam - and which must have presented a very unpleasant working environment in the early days. Pickers (often young boys or men who had been injured underground and who were only fit for surface work) were employed to inspect the coal as it travelled along the belts, breaking up larger pieces and removing any unwanted dirt and stone which was sent to the dirt disposal point for tipping on the adjacent meadows. The empty tubs were transported back to the shafts for return to the stalls in the underground workings.

The screens building graded the coal into various types which was then washed in a newly installed Simon Carves coal washing plant which had a capacity of 75 tons per hour. Following its grading into various types, (best house coal, second house coal and steam coal), the coal was then conveyed into hoppers which discharged it into a fleet of wagons for distribution via the railway network. The railway companies did not provide their own wagons; therefore, the colliery company purchased a fleet of 'private owner wagons'. These were initially lettered with the word **ROSSINGTON** in white letters edged in black with the words **MAIN COLLIERY CO LTD** in smaller type beneath. The whole wagon was painted grey and finished with its wagon number and the term **DONCASTER GNR**. Additional wagons were purchased in 1923 (a batch of 700), 1928 & 1935.

The whole surface plant had been equipped to handle a potential output of 1,500,000 tons of coal per year and to employ up to 4,000 men. However, despite a relatively successful start during the middle of the First World War, the colliery was looking to rapidly expand to meet this target, but this expansion was hampered by a shortage of men - as many were fighting in the army at the time and there was a lack of housing in the new village. In 1918, to facilitate these expansion plans, the capital of the colliery company was increased from £500,000 to £750,000 and 250,000 additional £1 shares were issued to the public.

With the outbreak of war, the Government had taken partial control of the mining industry and it wasn't until 1919, when control was passed back to the private colliery companies, that full expansion of Rossington Colliery could commence. In 1919, the colliery company recorded a profit of £22,434 although no dividend was paid to shareholders and all the profits were invested in building more houses. In 1920, a further profit of £4,091 was recorded and again it was decided to invest this money in more houses. The pit was fully developed and ready to produce its huge output, if only it could recruit more men and build more houses.

Above: *This large coal preparation plant was installed by Simon Carves Ltd in 1918 and is dominated by the huge concrete settling tank. A rake of the company's private owner wagons can be seen, together with an example from the associated Maltby Main Colliery and one belonging to Herbert Clarke Ltd, a London coal merchant. Note the two figures standing on the roof. Coal washing plants such as these usually generated waste material which was disposed of on the colliery tip. However, rather unusually for a pit of this size, Rossington Colliery never had an aerial ropeway to transport the unwanted spoil to a tipping site. In this case, such material was simply loaded into wagons which were driven by industrial locos up a steeply inclined line to the south of the pit to the tipping site, which eventually grew in height and volume.*

The colliery company were able to build 144 additional houses in 1919, 1920 & 1921 but the rapid rise in post war inflation meant that houses now cost 4 or 5 times as much to build compared to their pre-war levels. This was a national problem affecting the industrial areas of the country and causing concern in the Government. However, the problem was solved locally in 1922 when Rossington Main Colliery was one of six founding colliery companies that formed a house building organisation named The Industrial Housing Association Ltd.

Under a scheme devised by Sir Tudor Walters and Lord Aberconway, the Industrial Housing Association would be able to access government loans and subsidies in order to build quality houses designed by The Housing & Town Planning Trust – Sir Tudor Walter's own architectural practice. The colliery company subscribed £202,000 for shares in the Industrial Housing Association in exchange for the building of 955 houses in New Rossington during the period 1922-1926. In 1924, John Brown and Sheepbridge each provided a loan of £70,000 to Rossington

Main Colliery to pay for the additional housing for workers as well as providing £25,000 to purchase additional railway wagons. The house building scheme was a success, and this is reflected in the numbers employed by the colliery, now that additional houses had been built. In 1922, there were 1,506 employees, and this had increased to 2,317 by 1924 and 3,061 by 1930. This figure was matched by a dramatic rise in the population of Rossington – from 371 in 1911, to 3,029 in 1921, and to 9,547 by 1931.

In 1925, annual output passed 500,000 tons of coal for the first time, although this was still not enough to make a large profit and post war inflation was increasing the amount of capital required for the continued development of the colliery, a factor also effecting the neighbouring colliery at Maltby. The colliery was not profitable and failed to pay a dividend to shareholders due to problems with its underground development. A large profit could only be made on an output of a million tons of coal per year.

Following the General Strike in 1926, the Government was looking for voluntary amalgamations and consolidations within the mining industry in order to facilitate more efficient operations. Naturally, this was resisted in some areas, but Lord Aberconway saw the benefits of these proposals. Consequently, plans were drawn up for the amalgamation of Rossington, Maltby, Dinnington, Denaby & Cadeby collieries under a new company titled Yorkshire Amalgamated Collieries Ltd (henceforth referred to as YAC) which became effective from 27th March 1927, trading with a capital of £5,000,000. Basil Pickering became the agent to Rossington and Maltby Collieries; he was the son of W H Pickering, the Chief Government Inspector of Mines for Yorkshire and the North Midlands and who lost his life in the Cadeby Main Colliery disaster of 1912.

Each of the subsidiary colliery companies would continue to trade independently but its dividend would be paid to the parent company YAC. Shareholders would receive shares in YAC in exchange for their shares in the subsidiary companies, dividends being paid from the profits generated by the new parent company. Lord Aberconway took on the role of the first chairman of YAC, with Major Leslie from the Denaby & Cadeby Main Collieries Ltd and William Jackson of Sheepbridge Coal & Iron Company taking the roles of joint managing directors. They were joined by Sir Henry Norman, W H McConnel, F J Dundas, K R Pelly and Colonel Stobart who had all served on the boards of the various subsidiary companies. The aims of YAC were to develop the coalfield controlled by Rossington and Maltby Collieries; to eliminate the boundaries between the coalfields of the subsidiary companies, thus accessing 5,000,000 tons of coal; to establish joint selling arrangements and facilities for the joint purchase of materials; to increase coal output and the number of men employed following the development of Rossington and Maltby; and to pool financial resources with more economical working, treating and selling of the coal. It was proposed to borrow £500,000 to fully develop Rossington and Maltby pits.

The problems in developing Rossington Colliery in the 1920s were later revealed when YAC published an internal 'Report on Development'. The development of Rossington and Maltby had been under the control of mining engineers experienced in working the Top Hard coal seam of the Nottinghamshire and Derbyshire coalfields and it was found that this method of development was not suited to working the Barnsley coal seam of the Doncaster Coalfield. Consequently, it was necessary to develop working faces on different lines under new management. Considerable trading losses were made at the pit in the 1920s and it was not until 1929 when the developments implemented by the YAC had taken effect that the pit finally became profitable; the workforce then totalled over 3,000 and the yearly output was approaching the magical million tons - enabling a profit of £47,982 to be recorded in 1929.

Above: *Another postcard view published by Edgar Scrivens in the mid-1920s showing the surface layout at Rossington Colliery. The No 2 headgear (left) has been enclosed in a brick collar to aid the updraft and ventilation of the underground workings. Of note are the angled slots in the gable end of the two winding engine houses which each accommodated the different alignment of the winding ropes as they were wound around the winding drums.*

Above: *A postcard view published by Edgar Scrivens in the mid-1920s showing Rossington Colliery with the colliery offices on the left centre. This view is taken from Pit Lane (the western terminus of West End Lane) and shows the temporary railway line on the left which delivered building materials to a stock yard in the centre of the colliery village. On the left is a garage with sliding doors - possibly a bus proprietor's premises as the rear of a motor bus lettered T N Redfern can be seen.*

Below: *A similar view of Pit Lane issued on a postcard by James Simonton in the 1930s. No 2 Headgear has been partially enclosed to aid ventilation and to the immediate left can be seen the pit's water tower.*

It was always beneficial for a colliery to be connected to two different railway outlets but Rossington's only rail outlet had been via the branch line to the Great Northern Railway. This was despite the South Yorkshire Joint Railway, which had opened in 1909 and passed through the Rossington royalty a short distance to the north. In fact, the South Yorkshire Joint Railway had attempted to reach Rossington Colliery and an Act of Empowerment was obtained in 1913. However, since the pit was coming on line during the First World War, no work was done on this second railway outlet and the powers to construct this finally lapsed in 1931. Nevertheless, a second outlet to the colliery was opened the same year, this time by the LNER & LMS who opened a short branch leading northward from the pit though Potteric Carr to join the former Dearne Valley Railway at a westward facing junction amongst the nest of railway lines at Black Carr Sidings. This enabled Rossington coal to easily access trans-Pennine routes to the Lancashire and then the Irish Sea ports. However, this second branch line fell out of use during the Second World War and from that date onwards, all coal was transported out via the former Great Northern Railway branch line.

Above: *No mining community was complete without its brass band and in 1919, Rossington Main Colliery band was formed. This souvenir postcard by James Simonton shows the prize-winning band in 1924. In 1998 the band merged with Polypipe Brass Band to form Polypipe Rossington Brass Band but was sadly dissolved in 2004.*

Two postcards published in the early 1930s by Edgar Scrivens by which time Rossington Colliery had been absorbed by Yorkshire Amalgamated Collieries Ltd.

Above: *Pit Lane with the colliery offices on the left and the coal washing plant centre.*

Below: *A general view taken from the edge of Holmes Carr Wood showing the layout of the surface buildings* (Brian Brownsword Collection).

Above & Below:

The colliery commissioned its own promotional postcards which were ideal for acknowledging customer orders. This example was posted in 1931 to Messrs Fogwills of Guildford. Fogwills were based at Seed House in Guildford and their main business was the sale of seeds, although they also distributed coal to the town. In the 1950s, the NCB dropped the usage of the suffix 'MAIN' (an exception was Markham Main Colliery at Armthorpe which retained its suffix to distinguish this pit from Markham Colliery in Derbyshire). Consequently, Rossington Main Colliery was referred to as Rossington Colliery from the 1950s onwards. (John Ryan Collection)

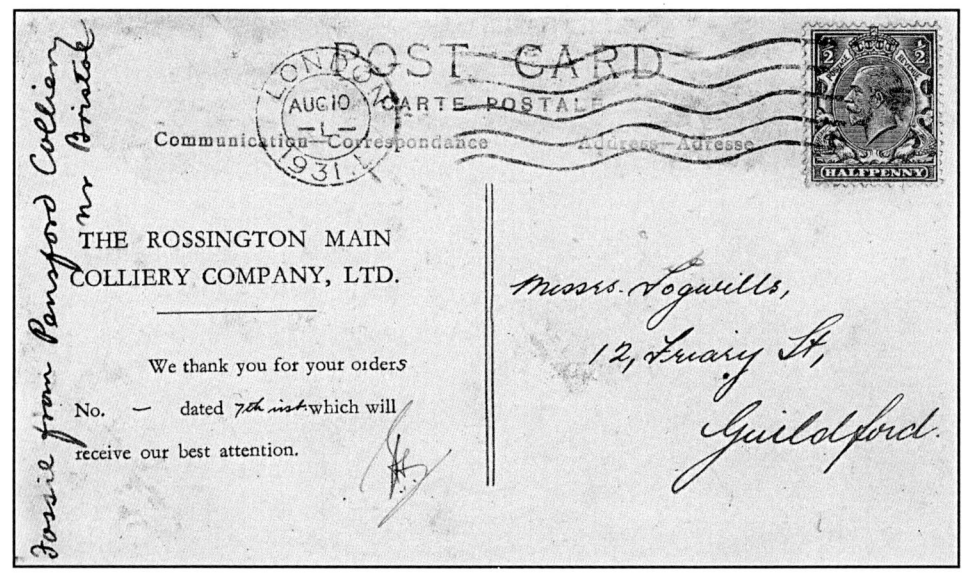

During 1933, YAC provided additional investment at Rossington when conveyors were introduced along the Barnsley seam longwall faces, which made the use of pit ponies largely redundant. On the surface, a huge new Baum coal washing plant was installed which had a capacity of 200 tons of coal per hour. This plant was built back-to-back with the earlier coal washery. These improvements finally saw the colliery produce 1,000,000 tons of coal per year during the 1930s.

However, concerned with the national overproduction of coal and consequent drop in price from a flooded market, the Government, empowered by the Mines Act (1930), imposed a quota system on every colliery in the country which led to considerable hardship in many of the country's mining districts. Rossington Colliery was allocated a relatively generous standard tonnage of 1,146,142 tons per year. Production above this figure would be met by severe financial penalties with any over-production being deducted from the following year's allocation.

Although the hardship experienced in Rossington with the onset of the depression wasn't as bad as that experienced in other colliery communities, for a period during the 1930s, the pit had to work one day on and one day off. Consequently, the workforce was on reduced hours and the number employed was gradually reduced from over 3,000 to 2,686 by 1938. Nethertheless, despite the harsh economic situation, the colliery was able to maintain a steady profit throughout the 1930s.

On 27th April 1936, YAC was reconstituted as Amalgamated Denaby Collieries Ltd which was formed to take over the colliery undertakings of the associated companies for the purpose of securing an increased annual standard tonnage allowance from the Government - as this would be higher if all the pits were owned by one company rather than individually. Lord Aberconway was appointed chairman of the new concern, and he revealed that YAC had spent £250,000 on developing Rossington Main Colliery.

Back in 1935, a pithead baths scheme had been approved at the pit and on Saturday 2nd April 1938, the new pit baths were opened by Captain Hodges, the Managing Director of Amalgamated Denaby Collieries and Tom Williams, the Labour MP for the Don Valley constituency. The new pithead baths were contained in a two storied building and contained 128 shower cubicles with accommodation for 2,688 men.

With the outbreak of war, the quota system and depression of the 1930s ended and Rossington Main Colliery was encouraged to achieve maximum production to assist with the war effort. However, despite mining being a protected occupation, many of the men enlisted causing a labour shortage and consequently war time production dropped; by 1947, only 2,150 men were employed at the pit. The national need for coal during the Second World War was addressed by the government in 1943 when they introduced numerous unskilled employees into the coal industry, for example 'Bevin boys' conscripted to work in the mines. Even though they had been reluctantly conscripted into the industry, the Bevin boys made a significant contribution to the nation's war effort. Many of the Rossington Colliery 'Bevin Boys' were housed at a large camp of Nissan huts at Intake in Doncaster.

Following the end of the Second World War, the newly elected Labour Government introduced a programme of nationalisation and on 1st January 1947, the British Coal Industry was nationalised with the formation of the National Coal Board (NCB). By way of compensation, the shareholders of Amalgamated Denaby Collieries received £5,621,200 for Rossington, Maltby, Dinnington, Denaby and Cadeby pits to pass into government control. Rossington Main Colliery became part of the NCB North Eastern Division (No 2 Doncaster Area).

During the 1950s, the NCB commenced a series of improvements and investments at Rossington Colliery, reflecting the introduction of increasing mechanisation nationally within the industry. This was coupled with a major house building programme in the village, with new estates provided by both the NCB and the local authority. At the pit, new tunnels and roadways were driven, and the underground rope haulage was replaced with a fleet of 100hp diesel locomotives. These transported coal in 3-ton capacity to the pit bottom. In 1953, the pit produced 1,011,629 tons of coal which brought the total output since 1917 to a huge 26,900,872 tons. A methane drainage scheme was introduced, tapping the gas from boreholes behind the Barnsley coal seam faces. The methane was pumped from the underground workings and piped ten miles away to fire the new coking plant at Manvers Main Colliery.

In 1956, the first workings were established in the Dunsil Seam and by 1958, the pit employed a workforce of 2,980 men who produced 1,051,000 tons of coal that year. A new Simon Carves coal washing plant with a capacity of 250 tons per hour was commissioned to handle the output from the Dunsil Seam. With the closure of Thorne Colliery due to water incursions in the shafts, around 600 miners were bussed in every day from Moorends near Thorne to work at Rossington Colliery.

In the early 1960s, a major restructuring scheme at a cost of £2,000,000 was introduced at the pit with the aim of introducing skip winding and replacing steam power with electric power. In 1963 a new headgear was erected above the original headgear at No 2 shaft and the following year the No 1 headgear was similarly replaced. The new steel headgears, at a height of 160 feet, were the tallest in Yorkshire. In 1964, both shafts were deepened to the Swallow Wood Seam at a depth of 928 yards. No 2 shaft was installed with a 12-ton capacity skip for coal raising whilst No 1 shaft was used for winding men and materials. Power loading was introduced at the various coal faces and 1964 saw the last hand filling of coal tubs.

The original Markham & Company steam winding engines were decommissioned and replaced with a pair of electrically powered friction winding engines. These were provided by the General Electric Company and positioned in new winding engine houses adjacent to the two shafts. The two redundant engine houses, dating from 1913 and 1915, were then used for storage. The modernisation scheme was completed in 1967 with the replacement of the original steam powered ventilation fan with a new electrically powered version. Production in the Dunsil Seam ceased in 1968 and all the Barnsley Seam output was conveyed to the No 2 pit bottom where it could be stored in two new underground bunkers prior to winding to the surface. The modernisation scheme was a success and in 1969, the workforce of 1,900 men produced 1,376,000 tons of coal, believed to be the record annual output achieved by the pit. Production regularly topped 20,000 tons of coal per week during the 1970s.

In 1971, a large concrete bunker known as a 'rapid loading bunker' was constructed to dispatch coal into trains that passed beneath the structure at a slow speed. These trains, typically complete with a rake of 42 standard NCB coal wagons, were known as 'merry-go-round trains' and conveyed coal to the new Central Electricity Generating Board power stations in the Trent valley and the Vale of York.

On 8th September 1972, a new 'Coalite' coal carbonising coking plant opened on a site to the north of the pit. The plant featured a battery of 20 coking ovens which were fed by conveyor from a huge concrete bunker that dominated the skyline. The Coalite plant, which manufactured smokeless fuel, was opened despite opposition from some in the surrounding area on the grounds of pollution. However, due to the decline in demand for smokeless fuel, the Coalite plant closed only four years later. However, the huge redundant concrete bunker was visible for a long time afterwards by drivers passing along the new M18 Motorway.

In the 1980s, there were still vast reserves of untapped Barnsley seam coal, particularly towards the east where the Dunsil and Barnsley seams merged to form a single seam 12 feet thick, and it was said that the coal extended eastwards as far as the North Sea.

During the yearlong Miners' Strike of 1984/5, the colliery was out of action, and scenes of industrial unrest occurred in the village. However, following the return to work, a new coal preparation plant was commissioned to handle the output from the combined seam and the older coal washing plant and screens were demolished and the NCB was renamed British Coal. Despite the closure of other collieries following the Miners' Strike, Rossington Colliery continued to operate as a profitable high-volume production unit and, in 1986, the colliery made a profit of £22,500,000. Therefore, it came as a surprise when British Coal decided to stop production at the pit on 26th March 1993. Rossington Colliery was put on a care and maintenance basis and with the forthcoming privatisation of the industry the colliery was offered to the private sector under licence.

Above: *A view of Rossington Colliery captured by the author in 1998 from the banks of the River Torne. Of note are the two winding engine houses (No 1 on the left with the datestone 1915 just visible in its gable and No 2 on the right with the datestone 1913 just visible in its gable). Unusually for a colliery where electrically power had superseded steam power, the redundant chimney survived until the end.*

However, although RJB Mining (UK) Ltd purchased most of British Coal's assets, Rossington Colliery was leased from the Coal Authority (the successors to British Coal) to RJB Mining on a ten-year lease and the colliery reopened on 21st March 1994 with 380 employees. In 1996, RJB Mining purchased the colliery and increased its operational licence for 25 years. The new owners continued to exploit the Barnsley Seam in the eastern district from a single mechanised coal face. On 14th July 2001, RJB Mining was restructured as UK Coal Ltd. However, the area of coal being worked was found to be vastly affected by geological faults which seriously hampered output and contributed to losses. An unsuccessful appeal for government funding to develop and equip a new coal face saw UK Coal announce that coal production would cease on Friday 31st March 2006. During its ownership under RJB/UK Coal, Rossington Colliery had produced 8,400,000 tons of coal.

The remaining 224 employees were engaged on salvage duties although some transferred to UK Coal's other pits at Kellingley and Thoresby. Demolition of the Rossington surface buildings commenced in 2007. For several years the site remained undeveloped, but in 2012, planning permission was granted to UK Coal's property division for the building of 1,200 houses adjacent to the colliery site. A scheme for a new link road from Junction 3 of the M18 Motorway to Rossington Bridge and Robin Hood Airport at Finningley, together with a spur road through the new housing estate to connect with West End Lane at New Rossington was devised. This also helped to open new employment opportunities with an inland railway freight depot (iPort) and Amazon warehouse distribution centres opening in the area.

In 2012, a scheme to restore the colliery site was awarded to RecyCoal who began working the colliery tip to extract small coal for selling to the electricity generating industry. The scheme is expected to produce 950,000 tons of coal with unwanted spoil being provided for the embankments of the new M18 link road. During this work, the colliery spoil heap was lowered considerably and is currently under landscaping. However, following a reduction in the price of coal, the scheme was suspended in 2015 and at the time of writing is awaiting further development.

On 14th August 1994, the Rossington branch of the National Union of Mineworkers and Rossington Parish Council unveiled a memorial to the men who had died at Rossington Colliery in the grounds of the Miners Welfare on West End Lane. The memorial plaque also remembers those who have died through industrial disease. During its operational life, the colliery claimed the lives of 92 men, the first fatalities being in 1917 when F Twigg and J Helps died whilst working at the coal face.

Following demolition of the colliery buildings in 2007, the two cast-iron date-stones from the winding engine houses dated 1913 and 1915 were positioned in a new memorial garden on McConnell Crescent, under a scheme devised by Rossington Parish Council. Work is presently ongoing with the reclamation of the pit site which it is hoped will become a country park complete with memorial garden. Hopefully this will form a fitting tribute to the local community.

Above: *The mining memorial in the grounds of Rossington Miners Welfare. During its operational life, Rossington Colliery claimed the lives of 92 men, the first fatalities being in 1917 when miners F Twigg and J Helps died whilst working at the coal face.*

Part 3
New Rossington

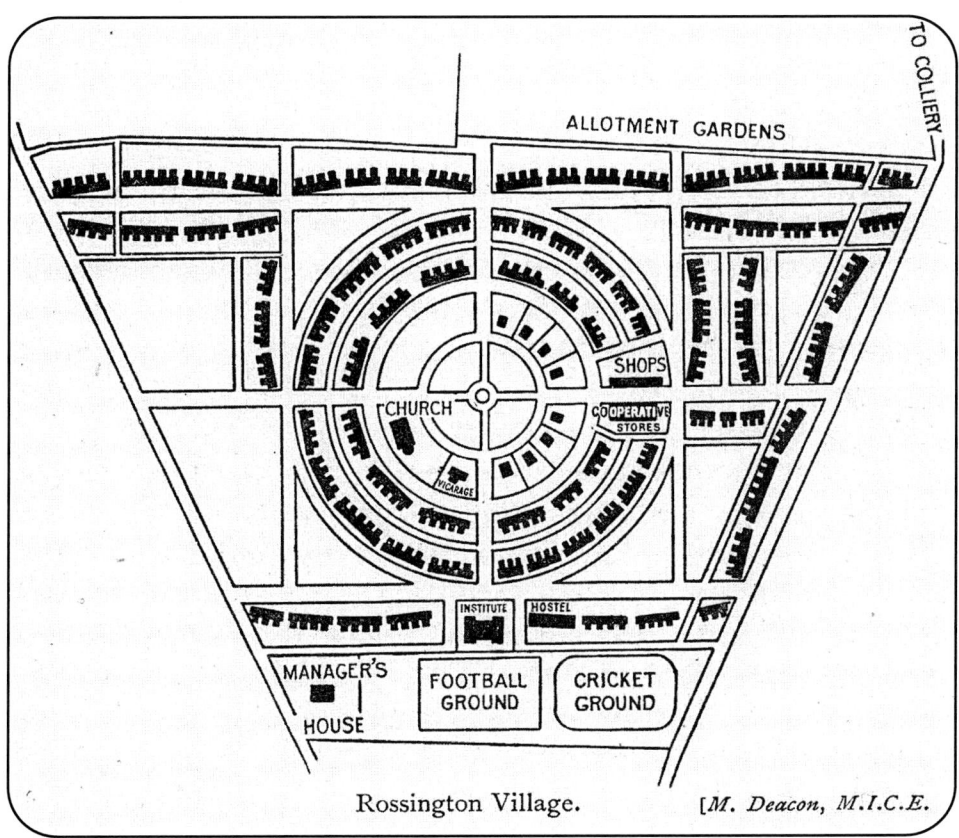

Above: *Maurice Deacon's plan for Rossington Model Village with Grange Lane on the left and West End Lane on the right. The plan clearly shows the central area of concentric circles, an idea recntly provided at Maltby Model Village. Restrictions during the First World War meant that only 466 houses plus the Manager's house, the shops, Co-operative stores and Church were completed by the time the pit commenced coal production in 1917. Reffered to as Rossington Colliery Village by the colliery company, the new settlement quickly gained the nicknames 'Rossie' and 'Rosso'.* (Plan From Bulman, 1920)

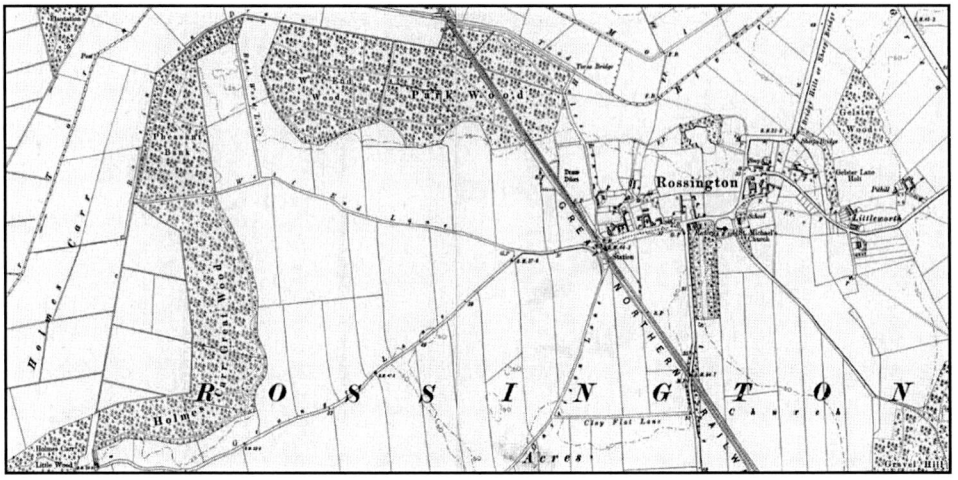

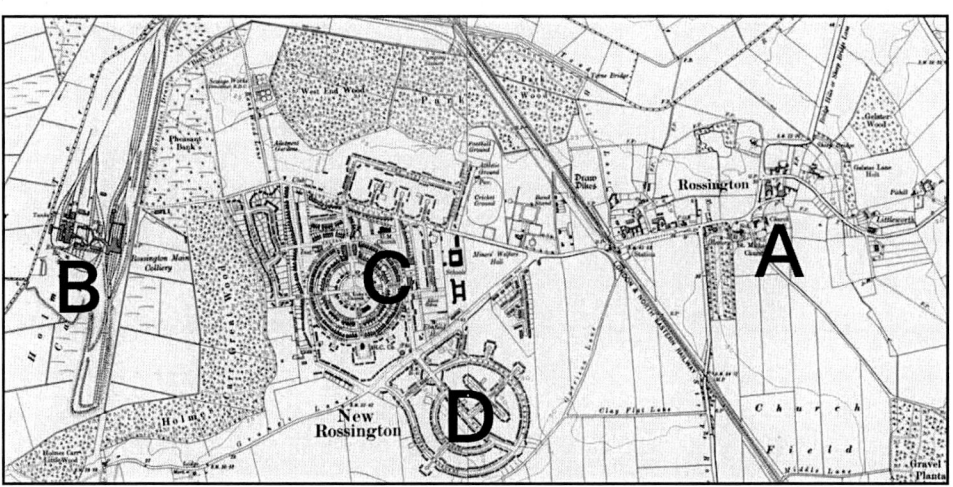

Top: 1901 1:2500 Ordnance Survey Map of Rossington.
Above: 1931 1:2500 Ordnance Survey Map of Rossington.

Two maps published 30 years apart showing the development of Rossington Main Colliery and the mining community of New Rossington. The 1901 map features the old estate village of Rossington to the east of the Great Northern Railway. Note the rural aspect of the landscape, dominated by agriculture and woodland and forming part of the Rossington Hall estate, the hall itself just off the map. The 1931 map shows the old estate village of Rossington (**A**) still largely unaffected by the development of the pit (**B**) on an isolated site to the east of Holmes Carr Great Wood. By this date, Rossington Main was employing over 3,000 men and producing a million tons of coal per year. However, the 1931 map features the 1,700 houses which form the mining community of New Rossington. The new village is separated from the pit by Holmes Carr Great Wood and from the older village by the railway line - by this date part of the London & North Eastern Railway. The mining community is dominated by the original 466 houses forming the concentric circles of the 'first circle estate' (**C**) with the 500 houses of the 'second circle estate' (**D**) to the south.

At the time of the 1911 census, the population of Rossington numbered 371, most of whom lived in the old village. From the parish church, a road led westwards to the level crossing by the railway station and continued the other side across the fields as a farm track named West End Lane to Holmes Carr Wood. Just over the level crossing, another farm track branched off to the south-west as Grange Lane, continuing for a mile to a farm known as Rossington Grange. Beyond Rossington Grange, the track continued over a bridge across the River Torne before reaching the village of Wadworth, some three miles away.

Therefore, apart from Rossington Grange, there were no buildings on the western side of the railway line. However, at the end of 1911, Maurice Deacon applied to Doncaster Rural District Council for permission to erect a temporary settlement of sinkers huts (known as 'Tin Town') on West End Lane near Holmes Carr Wood. These buildings, of wooden construction with corrugated iron roofs, arrived the following year to house the sinkers who would sink the shafts of the new pit. Presumably these huts were transported along the temporary railway line that had been constructed by the Great Northern Railway and were manoeuvred from the sidings on to a new site on West End Lane.

Reports from the sinking of Maltby Colliery state that most of the sinkers and their families transferred to the new settlement at Rossington when their work sinking the shafts at Maltby Colliery had been completed. They also brought their temporary settlement with them, consisting of the aforementioned accommodation huts, together with a food supplies hut, mess hall and a small wooden school that had been provided by the West Riding County Council. In 1916 when their work had been completed at Rossington, most of the sinkers and their families transferred to sink the shafts at Firbeck Colliery, although several of them chose to work at the new pit and several of their huts saw further use in Rossington.

The colliery company had purchased an 84-acre site from Richard Streatfield for the site of what they termed 'Rossington Colliery Village' but was named Rossington Model Village by the local press. (the first reference to the settlement as New Rossington did not occur until the 1920s). This new mining settlement would be in the wedge of land between West End Lane and Grange Lane and consisted of 1,000 houses, including two managers' houses, 16 officials' houses, church, church hall, chapel, shops, club, school and a recreation ground. In preparation for this, Mr Crabtree, the surveyor to the council, had organised the layout of sewers and a sewage works to the north of West End Lane. Although the colliery company would be providing the houses themselves, the responsibility for the water supply and sewerage lay with the local authority. However, the colliery company had sunk a borehole near the pit which provided adequate supplies of water and this was pumped to a tank for distribution around the village.

However, in 1912, the design for Rossington Colliery Village was drastically changed and new plans were drawn up by Maurice Deacon, this time for 848 houses plus a house for the colliery manager, together with two spaces allocated for chapels and another two spaces designated for "special purposes". Additional space was allocated for allotments, cricket ground, football ground and Miners Institute, together with a hostel which was intended to house single miners. The design for this new settlement would see many of the houses arranged around a series of four concentric circles; whilst on the straight roads, the houses would be aligned in gentle crescents with gardens and shrubbery filling the segmental gap in between. The circular layout was based upon that established a few years earlier at Maltby Model Village but improved on that design.

The building of Rossington Model Village was influenced by the Garden City Movement of the time and in 1912, prominent architect Sir Raymond Unwin published a pamphlet titled *'Nothing Gained by Overcrowding'* outlying the principles of the Garden City Movement. The Local Government Board recommended that *"cottages for the working classes should be built with wider frontages and grouped around open spaces which would become recreation grounds, they should have three bedrooms, a large living room, a scullery fitted with a bath and a separate water closet to each house"*. Raymond Unwin's influence and recommendations in house design were taken up by Lord Aberconway and Maurice Deacon in their plans for Rossington. However, it was also reported that conditions on the development of the village were placed upon it by Richard Streatfield.

The centre of the village would feature the rather grandly named "Aberconway Circus" after Lord Aberconway and was intended to feature a bandstand surrounded by parks and gardens, echoing that provided at Maltby Model Village. Around the innermost circle would be several semi-detached villas for officials and deputies, again mirroring the layout at Maltby. The next circle would feature blocks of larger houses with blocks of smaller houses being arranged around the outermost circle. It was stated in the local newspapers that

> ....."*as an example of town planning on a systematic scale, the new village of Rossington will win the attention of all interested in this great subject. There will certainly be nothing quite like it in England*"

Bisecting Aberconway Circus were streets generically named as King Avenue, Queen Avenue, Earl Avenue and Duke Avenue. The innermost circle however was formed from four streets named Fowler Crescent, Deacon Crescent, Ellis Crescent and Firth Crescent. The first two crescents were named after Frederick Fowler and Maurice Deacon, representing the Sheepbridge Company, with the second pair named after Charles Ellis and Bernard Firth, directors of John Brown & Company. The next circle, forming a service road or back lane between the innermost and outermost circles, received the generic names of Edgar Lane, Argyle Lane, Scarborough Lane and Victoria Lane.

The outermost circle was similarly split into four crescents. Two were named McConnel Crescent and Norman Crescent, after W H McConnel and Sir Henry Norman, directors of the Rossington Main Colliery Company and the Sheepbridge Coal & Iron Company; whilst the other two (Streatfield Crescent and Foljambe Crescent) were named after the two biggest landowners – James Streatfield of Rossington Hall and George Foljambe of Osberton Hall near Worksop. The circles were bounded by King George's Road and Queen Mary's Road, named after the King and Queen of the time, and their son Edward, the Prince of Wales, gave his name to Edward Road. Nelson Road and Wellington Road were named after military leaders Horatio Nelson and the Duke of Wellington. Finally, the many service or back lanes in the rest of the village received generic terms of Rufus Lane, Henry Lane, Granby Lane, William Lane, John Lane, Richard Lane, Albany Lane, Recreation Lane, Rutland Lane, Rosary Lane and Rookery Lane.

The streets remained the property of the colliery company and were laid out in 1913 and 1914. The main streets of the settlement were built with a width of 40 feet to ensure plenty of space. The colliery company purchased a small tipper wagon (registration WT5348) which was used for tipping ballast for road making. The back lanes behind the houses were used for refuse collection (known as 'scavenging' at the time) by the local authority and for the delivery of the miners' concessionary coal allowance.

The colliery company commissioned the builders Messrs Frederick Hopkinson & Company of Worksop to build the new village, although the houses and street layout were to designs prepared by Maurice Deacon. The Sheepbridge Coal & Iron Company had previously worked with Messrs Green Brothers of Old Whittington and Rotherham who had built colliery houses at Langwith and Dinnington. Green's designs had been adapted by the builder Herbert Mollekin at Maltby Model Village, and they were used again by Frederick Hopkinson for the building of Rossington Model Village.

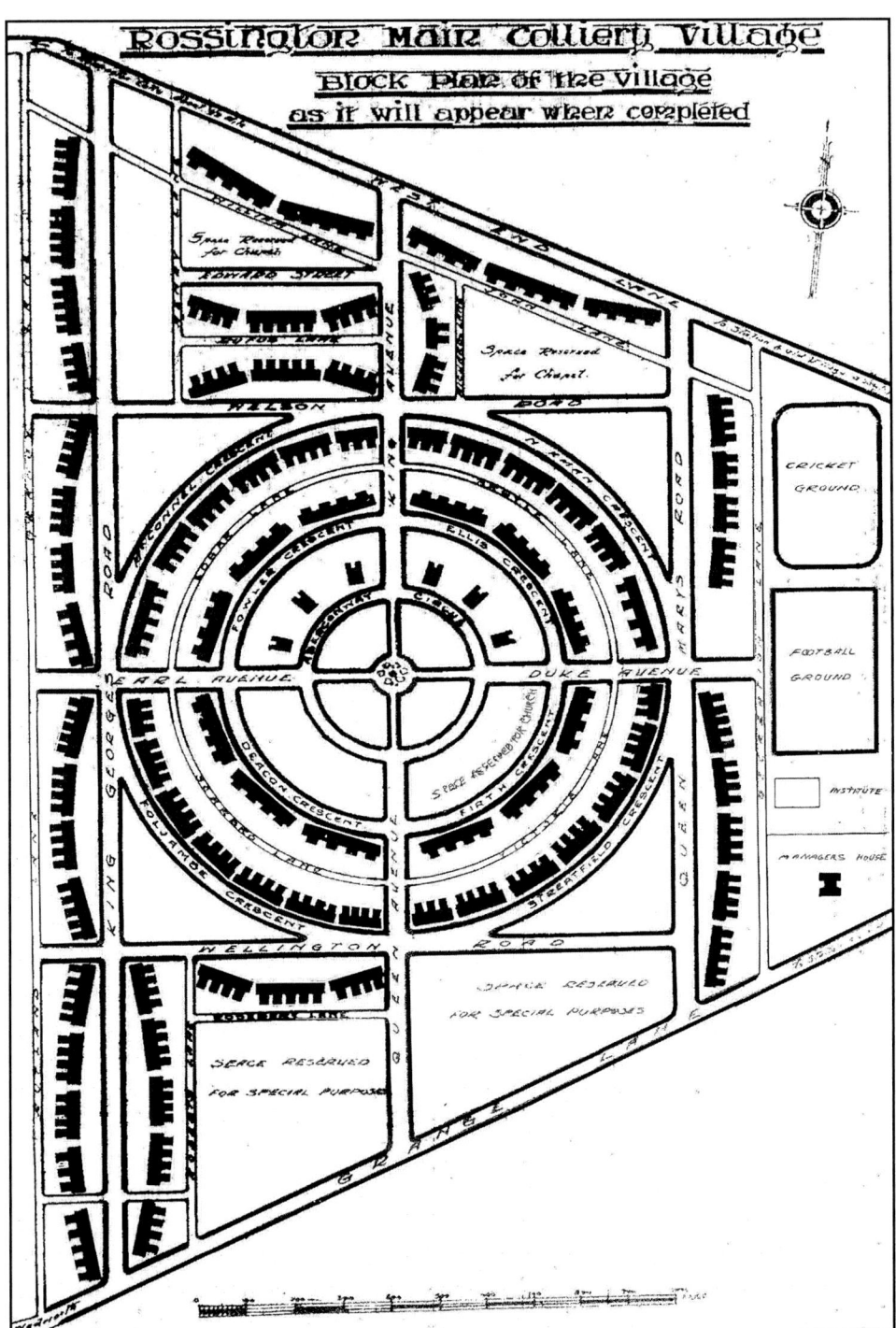

Opposite: *This revised block plan for 849 houses in Rossington Main Colliery Village featured in the 6th February 1914 issue of the Doncaster Chronicle and shows the series of concentric circles that we are familiar with today. However, this plan actually only depicts 716 houses plus 12 officials' houses and not all of these were built.*

Rossington is situated on the sandy soils of the 'Bunter Sandstones' and, although there was a small brickworks in the old village, this had long fallen out of use. Consequently, with no local clay deposits, there was a need to source vast quantities of bricks, not only to build the new village but also for use in lining the shafts of the pit and in constructing the surface buildings at the colliery. Consequently, a contract was signed with George Armitage & Sons Ltd who operated several brickworks located between Leeds and Wakefield. Bricks were brought by train to the colliery site, from which a temporary railway was laid along West End Lane which terminated in the vicinity of Aberconway Circus. This formed a temporary stockyard from which the bricks and building materials could be distributed. The first house constructed was a large detached villa on Grange Lane for Coningsby Phillips, the colliery manager. Plans for this house, known as Elmfield House, were submitted by Maurice Deacon to the local authority on 18th May 1912 and the building was completed on 22nd May 1913.

Attention then turned to the houses of the colliery village and these were built in various phases. On 9th May 1913, plans for 26 houses on West End Lane were submitted. This was followed by 94 houses on 29th November 1913, 44 houses on 28th November 1914, 170 houses on 17th April 1915, 36 houses on 22nd January 1916 and finally 96 houses on 8th July 1916. This brought the total number of houses to 466 when operations were suspended at the end of 1916 due to the Board of Trade taking temporary control of the mining industry. House building was deemed as non-priority despite Rossington Colliery producing its first coal on 17th July 1916. Consequently, work on the village was suspended and many of the proposed houses in the southern section along King George's Avenue, Queen Mary's Avenue and Wellington Road were never built, and neither were the large villas for officials in Aberconway Circus. The 466 houses constructed so far were grouped in blocks of four, six, eight and ten and there were three main types of house. They were referred to as 'cottages' by the colliery company, this being the common parlance of the day. The three cottage types consisted of:

Type 1 Cottage: These were the largest houses with a frontage of 20 feet with accommodation on the ground floor consisting of a front parlour with fire place, kitchen with range and hot water 'copper', scullery and pantry. Projecting from the rear of the kitchen was a single-story extension housing a bathroom, toilet and coal house. The upstairs accommodation comprised three bedrooms, (two of which had fire places) and a box room. A back garden, 40 feet in length, was also provided. Each Type 1 house cost approximately £185 to build and the rental charged was 6s11d/week including rates and taxes. 90 Type 1 properties were built on the innermost circle comprising Fowler, Deacon, Ellis & Firth Crescents.

Type 2 Cottage: These houses are identical in layout to Type 1, except the dimensions of the rooms are a little smaller as the frontage of the house measures 17 feet. Consequently Type 2 houses were cheaper to build at £165 each and the weekly rent was 6s9d. A total of 232 of these houses were built on West End Lane, King George's Road, Queen Mary's Road, Streatfield Crescent and Foljambe Crescent.

Type 3 Cottage: This was a smaller house with a frontage of 13 feet. Again, the downstairs accommodation was similar to the other types, although the room dimensions were smaller. Upstairs were two bedrooms whilst a projecting portion of the building housed a third bedroom above the scullery. The disadvantage of the full height rear extension was that it restricted light and sunshine from reaching the back rooms of the houses. Unlike the Type 1 and Type 2 houses, the Type 3 houses were provided with a smartly designed front porch. The weekly rent was 6s6d although the house cost is not stated, (presumably a little less than the Type 2 houses). A total of 144 Type 3 cottages were built on Norman Crescent, McConnel Crescent, Edward Street, King Avenue and Nelson Road.

The colliery company laid on water to the houses and the copper in the kitchen provided a hot water supply. Gas was supplied by the Bawtry & District Gas Company from their works at Bawtry, four miles away. The gas was paid for via a 'penny-in-the-slot' gas meter. Of note is the fact that the bathroom was provided in the downstairs of each house, on the understanding that the miner, arriving home in his 'pit muck', could head directly for the bath without traipsing dirt through the house to an upstairs bathroom.

The roof line of the front of all the houses was broken with the provision of a dormer gable above each of the bedroom windows. The dormer gable above each of the front bedrooms plus the porches of the Type 3 houses were finished with roughcast cement and black wooden beams – reflecting the architecture of the estate cottages in the old village. The front of each block of houses also featured two protruding bands of brickwork. The first was carried at the level of the windowsills of the bedroom windows. The second was set above the door and carried in a gentle arch over the parlour windows. The overall finish gave a smart appearance to each block of houses.

Above: *A postcard by James Simonton issued in 1915 (later issued in 1920 as number 44-35 in a series published by the Doncaster Rotophoto Company) featuring numbers 27 to 34 Foljambe Crescent. The overall smart appearance of these Type 2 cottages is evident from their dormer gables and brick bands.*

Below: *More Type 2 cottages in West End Lane showing the gentle crescent layout with the communal gardens and shrubbery. This has now been cleared and the space incorporated into the front gardens of the houses. This is another postcard view from 1915 captured by James Simonton.*

The initial inhabitants and the migration of labour into the new settlement requires further research. The first 26 houses built on West End Lane in 1913 housed men employed on carrying out underground development work. They came mostly from the surrounding area, with four from Maltby and eight from Stainton – reflecting the movement of the Maltby Colliery shaft sinkers as the 'tin town' at Maltby was in Stainton parish. However, the methods of recruitment for the colliery are unknown, but by 1917, 783 men were employed at the pit. As there were only 466 houses, presumably many houses catered for one or more lodgers or had father and son worked at the pit. An interesting aspect was the possibility that there was probably some considerable competition to recruit miners. Many men were away fighting during the First World War, and several of the other new Doncaster pits were recruiting at the same time. At Rossington, the colliery owners had the advantage of providing ready built accommodation which would have been attractive. Nevertheless, the migration of families into the area would benefit from more research, and men from many of the older coalfield areas – Staffordshire, Derbyshire, Nottinghamshire, County Durham, Northumberland – came to Rossington. It also is of note that Welsh accents were particularly prominent amongst the first inhabitants. Watching over this sea of colourful accents was PC Toyne of the West Riding Constabulary, and the colliery company allocated him a house at 20 Ellis Crescent.

As an exercise in town planning, the new Rossington Colliery Village was a partial success, particularly from the novel circular layout, demonstrating a hierarchical structure with the largest houses in the centre, followed by a ring of smaller houses with even smaller houses forming the outermost circles. However, it is a shame that the war interrupted its completion and despite the variety of house types, the simple terraced unit leant itself to an overall plainness, as Raymond Unwin's 'Arts and Crafts' recommendations were only adapted to a certain degree. In 1922, 'The Doncaster Regional Planning Scheme' was published by the famous town planner Sir Patrick Abercrombie and Doncaster architect T H Johnson. In this study, the authors comment on Rossington as follows *"its present method of planning leaves much to be desired, but the circular lay out, if carefully treated, will provide a village estate for a considerable population"*.

During the First World War, the Government had taken control of the British mining industry and, in order to encourage coal production for the war effort, pay and conditions had improved. However, following the end of the conflict, the Government handed control of the mining industry back to the private colliery owners who immediately implemented a 25% pay cut, resulting in a national strike, the first major period of industrial action affecting the Rossington miners.

During this dispute, the men were sadly defeated and reluctantly returned to work on the colliery owners' terms.

Now with full control of the village back in private hands, the colliery company decided to continue to develop the southern part of the model village, albeit to a revised layout. On 22nd November 1919, Maurice Deacon submitted plans for 14 houses on the western side of King George's Road. These were arranged in three blocks of four plus a single pair and were much larger than the pre-existing houses. They were very smartly presented properties with four bedrooms upstairs, and two living rooms, kitchen and bathroom downstairs. These houses were built in brick, possibly using existing stocks of Armitage bricks on the site. These houses also featured the two levels of protruding brick bands that were a feature of the original 466 houses.

However, nationally, the lack of house building was a major concern for the Government of the day, and it was estimated that a million houses needed to be built to satisfy the demand throughout the country. Details about rapidly soaring post-war inflation were outlined in a letter written by Frederick Hopkinson published in *The Times* on 25th January 1919. Hopkinson wrote that he used to build a six-roomed house, including land and roads, for £188, but at the present time it now cost £420, plus the cost of the land. He proposed that the industrial companies should form utility societies to undertake house building, enabling them to access government loans and subsidies to address the housing shortage. He stated that Messrs Hopkinson & Co were presently building colliery houses at Rossington, Maltby, Thurcroft, and Stainforth in South Yorkshire, plus at Pengam in South Wales. They were also preparing plans for the construction of three more mining villages, one in South Yorkshire, one in Lancashire and another on the new Kent coalfield.

Another contributary factor to the state of house building at the time was that the rail freight network was still in disarray following the end of the war and it was proving difficult to deliver bricks around the country. Consequently, the authorities encouraged builders to look at providing houses built from alternative materials. Therefore, on 8 July 1920, the colliery company submitted plans for 74 Dorman Long system-built *'Dorlonco'* steel framed houses. The Dorlonco semi-detached house had been designed in 1919 by architects Stanley Adshead, Stanley Ramsey and Sir Patrick Abercrombie to meet the government's request for housing. They were provided with a steel frame manufactured by Dorman Long & Company of Redcar and were neo-Georgian in style.

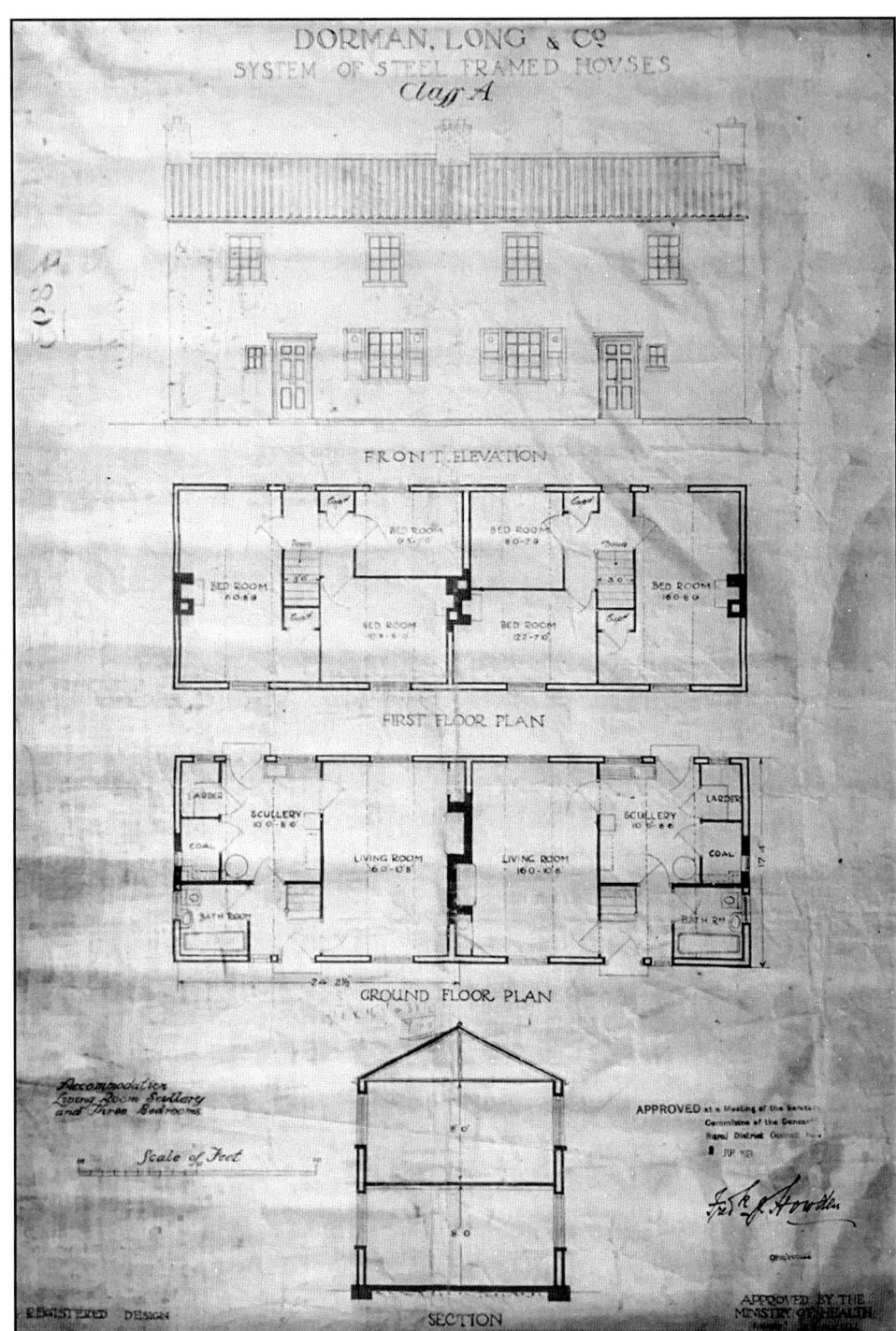

Opposite *Plan of steel framed Dorman Long houses as erected at New Rossington where these houses featured three bedrooms upstairs with the bathroom again provided downstairs. The walls were formed from steel laths or planks onto which cement render was applied to provide a light grey external finish.* (Reproduced with the consent of DMBC Doncaster Archives – part of Heritage Doncaster, Reference RD/DON/P/350).

Rossington Colliery purchased 36 pairs of Dorlonco houses and positioned them on the southern sides of Foljambe Crescent and Streatfield Crescent, Queen Mary's Road and Grange Lane. The plan for laying out Wellington Road was abandoned, and the houses were also arranged around three squares – Banks Square, Skipwith Square and Whitaker Square. The naming of these squares reflected three additional leaseholders – Elizabeth Banks of St Catherine's Hall; Sophia Skipwith of Loversall Hall; and Benjamin Whitaker of Hesley Hall.

More than 10,000 Dorlonco houses were built in the whole country, and, elsewhere in South Yorkshire they were constructed at Rawmarsh, Maltby, Stainforth and Kirk Sandall. However, over time they suffered from the deterioration of the steel frame and cement render leading to structural problems. If this defect was caught early enough and the houses were reskinned with bricks, this would allay the problem, but at Rossington, the deterioration ultimately led to their demolition at the end of the 1970s.

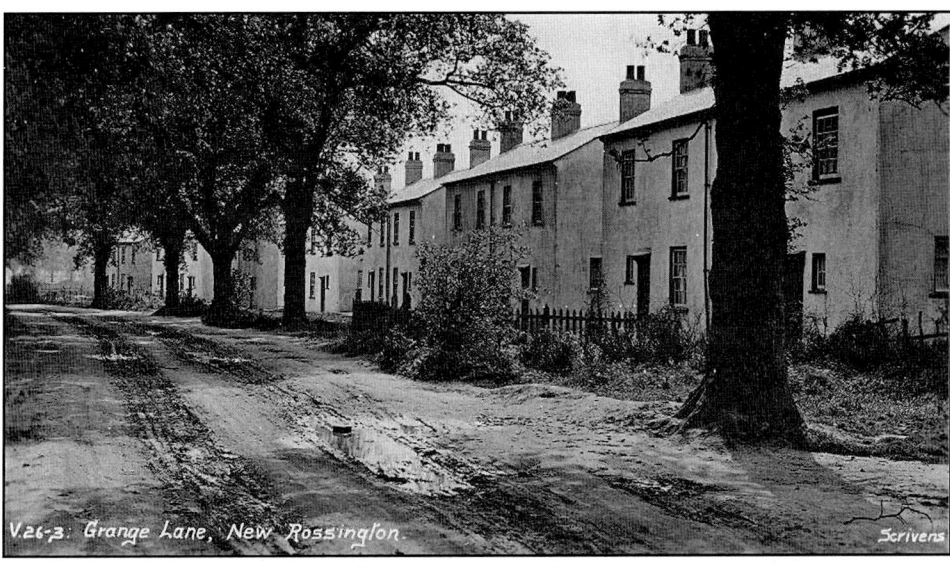

Above: *Edgar Scrivens photographed these Dorlonco houses on Grange Lane in the mid-1920s. They were demolished in the late 1970s.*

On 23rd November 1920, plans were submitted by F Contrill on behalf of the colliery company for 12 brick-built houses to be constructed on the eastern side of King George's Avenue – arranged in two pairs and two blocks of four. Around this time, King George's Avenue was extended diagonally to link up with Grange Lane. These houses lacked the two protruding brick bands of earlier designs.

On 2nd July 1921, the colliery company submitted plans for an additional 44 houses. These were built in pairs and blocks of four. 30 houses were arranged either side of the extension of King George's Road and 14 were erected on the eastern side of Queen Mary's Road. They were identical to those provided by F Contrill the previous year, except they featured the two protruding brick bands with patterned or ridged bricks.

The provision of 144 houses of various designs during 1919, 1920 & 1921 brought the total number of colliery houses to 610 (plus the house for the manager). However, the pit was wishing to expand and attract more men to work in order to produce the magic million tons of coal per year from which a profit could be made but the lack of housing was holding them back. This was a national problem throughout the industrial areas of the country and was causing politically concern at the time. In 1918, the Government commissioned Sir Tudor Walters MP to produce a report into the design, layout and development of council housing, recommending the building of houses to larger dimensions and higher standards than before, by accessing loans and subsidies from the Government's Public Works Board. This led to the formation of the 1919 (Addison) Housing Act.

Local authorities were now able to provide their own council housing. However, Tudor Walters was a fellow Liberal MP with Lord Aberconway and the late Sir Arthur Markham. Tudor Walters had designed housing in 1920 for Hickleton, Bullcroft and Markham Main pits. Consequently, in 1922, following the loss of his seat at the general election, Tudor Walters and Lord Aberconway decided to form the Industrial Housing Association Ltd an organisation designed to provide colliery houses built to the standards of the 1918 Tudor Walters Report and designed by his own architectural practice – the Housing & Town Planning Trust.

The Industrial Housing Association would build 35 colliery villages throughout England and Wales and its first scheme was focussed on Rossington where, from 1922 to 1926, 955 houses would be built on behalf of the colliery company. The Industrial Housing Association purchased various sites from Richard Streatfield and commenced building operations. The colliery company subscribed for £202,000 in shares in the Association to pay for the building of the houses.

Above: *Another mid-1920s postcard by Edgar Scrivens featuring the junction of Foljambe Crescent and King George's Road, showing five different types of housing. 1) Type 2 Cottages erected in 1915. 2) Dorman Long Dorlonco steel framed houses from 1920. 3) Houses designed without banding by F Contrill 1920. 4) A solitary block of four houses built by The Industrial Housing Association in 1924 at the corner of King George's Road. 5) Parlour Cottages with brick bands designed by Rossington Colliery in 1919.*

On 22nd October 1922, work commenced on constructing 220 houses on a 22-acre site to the north of West End Lane. This plan was amended to 212 houses provided in pairs and blocks of four, and Cambridge Street, York Street, Lincoln Street, Newark Street, Ely Street and Oxford Street were laid out. These streets, together with Grantham Road in the next development, were named after railway stations on the Great Northern Railway (York, Newark, Grantham) and the Great Northern & Great Eastern Joint Railway (Lincoln, Ely, Cambridge). Finally, if you have a Cambridge Street then you must have its university rival, Oxford Street! On 13th January 1923, plans for 93 more houses were submitted, mostly to fill undeveloped spaces in and around the original village. 43 houses were provided on Grantham Street, 26 houses were built at the north of King George's Road and on Edward Street, and 11 pairs of large semi-detached houses were provided for deputies around Aberconway Circus - now renamed as The Circle. These latter houses reflected the original plan to provide 16 officials' houses at this location. Additionally, on 30th June 1923 a detached Doctor's house and surgery was provided in The Circle for Doctor Kane, the pit Doctor. Around this time a single block of four houses was also built on King George's Road amongst earlier housing from 1920.

Above: *The first phase of housing provided by the Industrial Housing Association formed a development of 212 houses built in 1922 along York Street, Cambridge Street, Oxford Street and three cul-de-sacs named Lincoln Street, Newark Street and Ely Street. This Edgar Scrivens postcard from 1930 features Type A3 houses on York Street.*

Below: *Allenby Crescent in the second circle estate was built in 1923/4 and was named after Field Marshall Edmund Allenby. This is another in a series of postcards photographed by Edgar Scrivens in 1930.*

Above: *Central Drive bisected the second circle estate, and at the cross roads with Aberconway Crescent and Junction Road, the Industrial Housing Association arranged a group of Type L corner houses which form an octagonal shape when viewed from above.*

Below: *James Simonton has captured the colliery company estates department constructing garden walls and pavements on Haig Crescent. This area was often known as 'Little Wigan' and one Rossington lad, working for Wildsmiths Newsagents, would collect newspaper money from the Haig Crescent houses, entering the payments into his notebook with Little Wigan written on the front.*

On 12th January 1924, attention turned to building 'the second circle estate' to the south of Grange Lane. This featured 500 houses forming the streets named Central Drive, Aberconway Crescent, Allenby Crescent, Haig Crescent, Junction Road, Whitby Road, Cross Street and Tudor Street. Of these streets, Allenby Crescent and Haig Crescent were named after the army generals Viscount Edmund Allenby and Douglas Haig. In compensation for having Aberconway Circus renamed as The Circle, Lord Aberconway gave his name to Aberconway Crescent. Finally, the architect of the whole development, Tudor Walters, gave his name to Tudor Street.

On 1st May 1926, plans were drawn up for the final development of 147 houses forming the Holmes Carr Estate, located between Holmes Carr Wood and King George's Road and consisting of Holmes Carr Road and Holmes Carr Crescent. As part of this development, 20 houses for deputies and officials were built facing West End Lane.

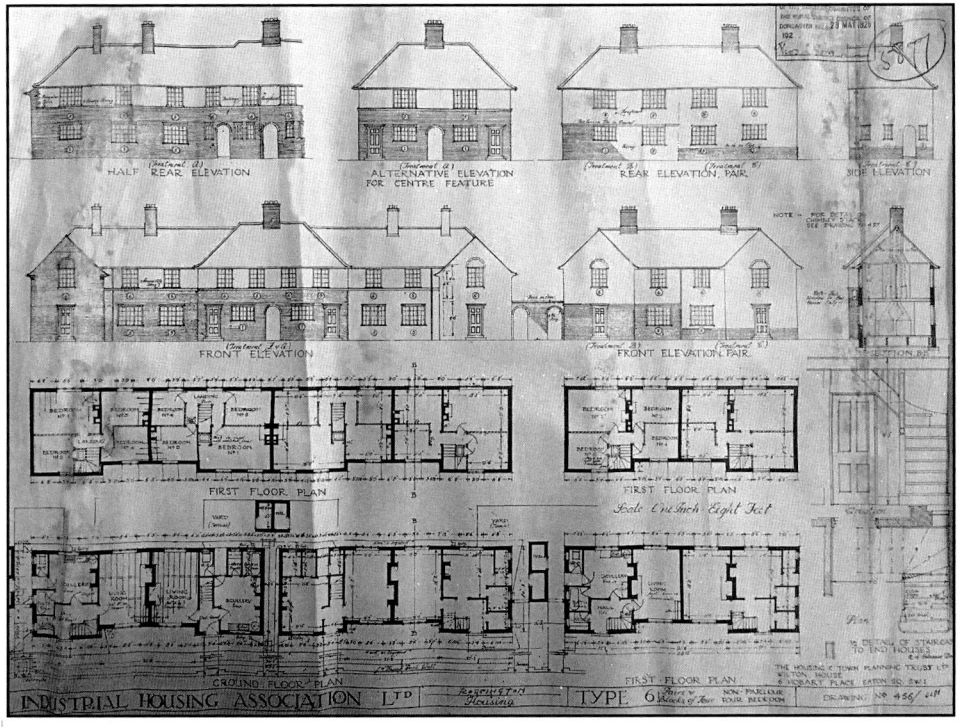

Above: *The Type 6 non-parlour four-bedroom house (and its mirror image) could be arranged into a block of four and a semi-detached block, as shown in the plans above which were approved by the local authority on 29 May 1926. These houses were built on Holmes Carr Road and Holmes Carr Crescent.* (Reproduced with the consent of DMBC Doncaster Archives – part of Heritage Doncaster, Refence RD/DON/P/346).

The houses produced by the Industrial Housing Association were built in various blocks of 2, 3, 4, 5 & 6 with a block of 10 being provided on Holmes Carr Crescent. Again, the bricks were delivered to the area by train – mostly from the London Brick Company's brickyards near Bedford and Peterborough. Several brick types were used including smart looking rustic bricks on some of the houses fronting West End Lane. The houses featured a variety of different types and were built for around £450-£500 each. They were typically let at a rent of 8s/week. On Grange Lane and Central Drive, some rather expensive angled blocks were built, a feature praised by Sir Patrick Abercrombie when he reviewed the scheme.

The addition of 955 houses provided by the Industrial Housing Association brought the total number of colliery houses calculated in this study to 1,566 - although the Rossington Main Colliery Company 1926 AGM states 1,571 houses, were now owned. The discrepancy in figures may come from including other individual properties owned by the colliery company but not listed in the records; for example, a building near the Manager's House named the Bungalow which was also owned by the colliery company.

However, in 1927, Doncaster Rural District Council provided Rossington's first council houses, when 58 houses were laid out on the Grangefield Estate development on Grange Lane. This consisted of houses in pairs and blocks of four, built along Grangefield Avenue, Grangefield Terrace and Haslam Road – the latter probably named after T E Haslam, the colliery company secretary. A further 12 houses were added in 1929 but plans for an additional 26 houses were abandoned and the estate remained incomplete until after the Second World War. Unlike the houses built by the colliery company, the council houses were available to anyone – not solely miners.

The construction of over 1,000 houses during the period 1922-1927 saw the pit undertake a huge recruitment drive and, by 1931, the population of Rossington had increased to 9,547. By this time, the colliery company was employing 3,000 men who were producing a million tons of coal per year and thus the pit was finally profitable, after nearly 20 years of development. In the village many different accents could be heard originating from other parts of the country, and certain areas gained nicknames on account of this. For example, Grantham Road and parts of the second circle estate were known as 'Little Wigan' and the Holmes Carr Estate was called 'Geordieland'. A report in June 1927 stated that 200 men had left the Durham Coalfield to seek a new life in Rossington – possibly accommodated in the Holmes Carr development.

Two views of New Rossington captured by Edgar Scrivens in the mid-1920s.

Above: *Norman Crescent featuring the Royal Hotel on the right. In the distance, the village market can be seen in full swing.*

Below: *The centre of the village was originally named Aberconway Circus but was renamed The Circle when the Industrial Housing Association completed the scheme with these large semi-detached properties for colliery officials. St Luke's Church is on the right.*

Two views of New Rossington captured by James Simonton in the 1930s.

Above: *Type 3 Cottages on Kings Avenue, with their distinctive front porches. Many enterprising miners' wives turned their front rooms into small shops and this area still forms a small shopping parade today.* (Brian Brownsword Collection).

Below: *Queen Mary's Road looking south towards the water tanks. The 'banded' houses on the left were built in 1921 and the village post office moved into the newly constructed block of shops on the right in 1930.*

The men who designed and built New Rossington

Left: *Lord Aberconway was born Charles Benjamin Bright McLaren on 12th May 1850 and died on 23rd January 1934. In 1874 he became a barrister and served as the Liberal MP for Stafford (1880-1886) and Bosworth (1892-1910). He followed in his father-in-law's footsteps into industry, becoming Chairman of John Brown & Company, The Metropolitan Railway, The Tredegar Coal & Iron Company and The Rossington Main Colliery Company. In 1902 he was created a baronet, and this title was elevated to Baron Aberconway of Bodnant in 1911. His home at Bodnant Gardens was subsequently gifted to the National Trust in 1949.*

Centre: *Maurice Deacon was born on 11th November 1850 and died on 25th September 1941. After serving as an engineer and surveyor for the Coal Commission, he managed collieries in Wales and Derbyshire before joining the Sheepbridge Coal & Iron Company in 1896, rising to the post of Managing Director. He also served as Managing Director of Rossington Main Colliery Company. A Member of the Institute of Civil Engineers, he oversaw the development of the pits and colliery villages at Dinnington, Maltby and Rossington. He resigned his directorships in 1924 due to ill health and retired to his home, Chase Cliffe at Whatstandwell in Derbyshire.*

Right: *Sir John Tudor Walters was born in 1868 and died on 16th July 1933. He was elected as the Liberal MP for Sheffield Brightside from 1906 to 1922 and also served as Paymaster General. His 1918 Tudor Walters Report led to the establishment of the 1919 Housing and Town Planning Act which empowered local authorities to create council housing. He ran his own personal architectural practice - the Housing & Town Planning Trust – as well as creating the Industrial Housing Association in 1922, designing 955 houses in New Rossington.*

The one man missing from the above and whose firm carried out the actual construction work is Frederick Hopkinson of Worksop, who was responsible for the building of most of New Rossington and several other colliery villages in South Yorkshire and further afield in Kent and South Wales. Hopkinson's building concern must have employed several hundred people and despite the availability of plenty of work, it is rather surprising that the company went into liquidation in 1927. A man named Frederick Hopkinson then opened a butchers shop in the village - is this the same person? Did he take up residence in the place he built?

In 1927, the Bawtry & District Gas Company provided street lighting and the colliery company fixed street names to the houses – these featured white lettering on a black background. That year, the colliery company upgraded the water supply and erected 'the tanks' – a large iron water tower at the southern end of Queen Mary's Road.

The expanded population, ultimately by 1927 housed in over 1,800 colliery-owned or council-owned properties, created a totally new settlement now referred to as New Rossington. This meant that a whole host of services would be needed in the form of shops, schools, pubs, clubs, places of worship, and leisure facilities together with transport connections to surrounding towns. With the building of Rossington Model Village, provision had been made for a church, a chapel, a school and a Miners' Institute, but the first need for the new populace would be shopping facilities.

In the old village of Rossington in 1912, Joseph Dickinson ran the sub Post Office and Arthur Adams owned a small shop, although these would be inadequate to serve the new mining community 'on the other side of the tracks'. The sinkers had a supply hut in their 'tin town' and this would have been served by visiting tradesmen - although it is highly likely that frequent poaching expeditions were mounted as well as the raiding of local fields for potatoes and turnips!

However, the first purpose-built shops opened in 1915 when Frederick Hopkinson constructed a large building for the Doncaster Mutual and Industrial Co-operative Society on King's Avenue, and this was followed by the opening of four shops on the opposite side of the road. This served as the shopping centre for the new village and was supplemented by small front room shops run by enterprising miners' wives in some of the houses on King's Avenue to the north. This shopping centre served the village until 1923 when Frederick Hopkinson extended the shopping parade with eight additional shops along Kings Avenue; the parade then continued around the corner into Fowler Crescent.

In 1924, the Industrial Housing Association provided four 'cottage shops' on Grange Lane, with the idea being that they could easily be converted into houses if no longer required as shops. In 1926, the General strike brought hardship to the village and a soup kitchen was established behind the Co-operative Stores. The soup kitchen also distributed 'dole bread' to the striking miners and their families. At some time in the 1920s, a market had become established on Norman Crescent, and, on 31st March 1928, builder H J Hepworth submitted plans for another shopping parade – subsequently 9 shops were built along Nelson Road, creating another shopping centre for the village. Additional shops and a Post Office were built in 1930 at the junction of Streatfield Crescent and Queen Mary's Road.

The South Yorkshire Coalfield Church Extension Committee was formed on 21st April 1910 to further the spiritual needs of the new colliery settlements; the committee consisted of landowners, colliery owners, the clergy and miners. At Rossington, the colliery company provided a free site for a new church, parsonage and church hall and the Committee commenced raising the finance required. The colliery company granted £50 per year towards the stipend for the incumbent for the first three years. Richard Streatfield of Rossington Hall donated £1,500 towards building costs whilst Mr Whitaker of Hesley Hall provided a donation of £200 with the Sheffield Diocesan Fund contributing £350. The funds went towards building St Luke's Church, a handsome brick structure built in the Italianate style.

Above: *Although slightly over-exposed, this James Simonton postcard from the 1950s is included for its interest, showing the shopping parade on Nelson Road with the United Methodist Church in the distance. Established in 1896, Melias Ltd was a chain of grocers and tea dealers with branches throughout the country; it unfortunately succumbed to the growth of the supermarkets in the 1960s.*

St Luke's Church was designed by Sprake & Sons of Doncaster to designs by the architect F Norman Masters and the church opened ten months after the stone laying ceremony. This quick turnaround was because the Committee had designed the concept of 'production line churches' and the building at Rossington is similar (but not identical) to other churches provided by the Committee at Maltby, Bentley and New Edlington.

On 18th October 1916, the Bishop of Sheffield performed the dedication service and the architects presented a gold key to Miss Streatfield to unlock the door. The first curate appointed was Reverend E E Johnson, who in addition to his clerical duties, worked 6 shifts per week at the pit to assist with the war effort. At the time, The Circle was used as a stockyard for building operations and was filled with piles of bricks, sand and gravel. Consequently, Reverend Johnson laid duck boards and oil lanterns to light the way to the church from King's Avenue. During 1916, Reverend Johnson worked six shifts per week at the pit and he subsequently signed up to fight in the war, but, in 1917, he sadly lost his life from influenza on the battlefields of France.

Above: *St Luke's Church, depicted on a mid-1920s postcard published by Edgar Scrivens. On 8th December 1915, Miss Annette Streatfield was to perform the stone laying ceremony. However, the weather was so atrocious that the ceremony had to be moved to the Co-operative Hall. St Luke's served as a daughter church to St Michael's Church until 1956 when a separate parish was created. St Luke's was awarded Grade II listed building status on 28 April 2008.*

The Parsonage opened soon afterwards, and the colliery company provided an old sinker's hut to use as a parish hall. This survived for 18 years until it was replaced by St Luke's Church Hall which was opened on 4th August 1934 by Mr W B M Jackson, the managing director of the colliery company.

In 1922, the Salvation Army opened new premises on West End Lane, again utilising a former sinkers' hut. It was felt that a new cemetery was required and on 16th September 1922, the Bishop of Sheffield consecrated one on an isolated site on Grange Lane.

A site for a Roman Catholic Church was given by the colliery company amongst the Dorlonco houses in Skipwith Square and on 31st July 1928, the first stone was laid for this building. On 4th August 1929, the Bishop of Leeds performed the opening ceremony of Christ the King Roman Catholic Church and the adjoining Presbytery.

Above: *In 1920, the colliery company donated a site on Nelson Road and gave £100 towards the building of a Methodist Chapel and Sunday School in a scheme which cost £4,500. The United Methodist Sunday School was opened on 2nd June 1921 by Mrs Maclaurin of Sheffield and Mrs Richardson, the wife of the colliery manager. The building was extended in 1928. The last service was held on Sunday 24th February 2019, following which the chapel sadly closed due to the dwindling congregation. However, there is currently a campaign to save the buiking for community use.*

The sinkers had brought a small wooden school from Maltby but, in 1915, the West Riding County Council provided temporary schools for the new mining village on a site off West End Lane. There were at least two wooden huts and it is likely that these were brand new buildings rather than re-appropriated former sinkers' huts. The school was, unsurprisingly, christened 'The Wooden Hut School'. The rapidly expanding population resulted in the wooden hut schools being replaced by larger premises which opened on 8th November 1922. This new school was christened 'the brickies' and was provided by the West Riding County Council, featuring classrooms arranged around a quadrangle, which was a popular layout at the time.

The educational organisation was subsequently restructured: the school built in

1922 became Rossington County Primary School (later Pheasant Bank School) and that provided in 1929 became Rossington County Secondary Modern School (later Holmes Carr School).

Above: *Following the completion of the Industrial Housing Association's additional 955 houses, the West Riding County Council provided additional schools on a site to the south of 'the brickies'. The new 'pit school' was opened on 14th September 1928 at a cost of £18,204. The school was built by the firm of A Bull & Company of Doncaster and provided accommodation for 240 boys and 280 girls and was designed to allow extension to accommodate 280 more children. As part of this development, four houses were built on Grange Lane for teaching staff. This view by James Simonton shows the schools from Grange Lane.*

It is well known that mining is thirsty work, but the proposed Miners' Institute had not yet been built. There was no public house in Old Rossington and the inn at Rossington Bridge had closed many years before, so for the first few years of its life, New Rossington was eseentially a dry village. However, on 13th March 1920, Frederick Hopkinson submitted plans for a large licensed premises named the Royal Hotel. In 1921, the forerunners of the British Legion (the New Rossington Comrades of the Great War) opened a club on West End Lane using an old sinkers' hut. On 8th September 1930, the wooden hut was replaced by a purpose-built brick premises opened by the 6th Earl of Harewood. A third licensed premises opened in 1923 when the colliery company moved another former sinkers' hut to a piece of land off McConnel Crescent. This became the Miners' Institute and an additional adjoining wooden hut was used as a billiard hall. However, eight years later, the Miners, Institute moved into purpose-built premises on Nelson Road which became known as the 'Top Club'.

Above: *The Royal Hotel was opened in 1921 by Mr Deacon on the site of the proposed Miners Hostel. The first licensee of 'The Royal' was Mr J Farnsworth and the huge building even featured a stable block to the rear. Reflecting the national decline in drinking socially, the Royal Hotel closed in 2006 and was demolished shortly afterwards. The site is now occupied by a new retirement home. This postcard was issued by Lawrence of Doncaster when Alfred Wigmore was proprietor.*

Below: *The original plan for New Rossington compiled by Mr Deacon in 1912 featured a Miners' Institute, possibly to a similar design as the institutes provided at Maltby and Dinnington. However, it wasn't until 1930 that building commenced with Rossington Miners' Institute.*

One of the most important results of the Mining Industry Act of 1920 was the establishment of the British Miners' Welfare Fund, the income of which was used for *'purposes connected with the social well-being, recreation and conditions of living of workers in or about coal mines'*. The fund received its income from a levy of a penny on every ton of coal produced, in order to improve facilities in the mining districts. In 1924, the Miners' Welfare Fund purchased a site on West End Lane from Richard Streatfield for the laying out of Rossington Miners' Welfare at a cost of £6,890. The scheme consisted of a hall to accommodate 500 people, four reading rooms, a library and a caretaker's house. Outside facilities comprised a cricket pitch with cycle track and pavilion, a football ground, two bowling greens and three tennis courts. Additionally, parks and gardens were also provided as well as a playground called the Children's Corner which had swings and a paddling pool. On 16th May 1925, the scheme was opened by Mr W B M Jackson, the Managing Director of the Rossington Main Colliery Company. In 1930, the architects T H Johnson of Doncaster provided a highly ornate bandstand, complete with clock and weather vane.

In the 1920s another club opened when a wooden hut was positioned at the corner on King George's Road. This became the Officials' Club and two other huts were added to this location. Finally, in 1932, another public house opened at the junction of West End Lane and Grange Lane when Tenants Brewery opened the Station Hotel. However, this pub was always referred to as *"the new 'un"*.

Back in 1916, the first miners formed a union – the Rossington branch of the Yorkshire Miners Association - itself a member of the Miners Federation of Great Britain. The union went on to represent their members rights, in what could be a constant battle with the ruthless private colliery owners, and continually pressed them to improve the facilities, both at the pit and in the village. One of the first achievements of the union was to recruit a pit doctor. This was of course prior to the formation of the National Health Service, at a time when summoning the nearest private doctor from Bawtry would result in expensive medical fees. Consequently, in exchange for a contribution of 4d/week deducted from their wages at source, the newly qualified Doctor Patrick Kane arrived at Rossington and the colliery company gave him two adjoining houses on Queen Mary's Road - one for his private use and the other to use as a surgery. Doctor Kane married a nurse from Doncaster Infirmary Hospital and moved to a Rossington, which, he said *"looked like the wild west"* on account of the bleak and pioneering aspect of the new settlement. In 1924, he moved to a new detached house and surgery in The Circle and in the 1930s he was joined by Doctor Ritchie and Doctor Grafdyke. Doctor Kane worked in medicine until his retirement in 1974.

Rossington Miners Welfare

*Work commenced in June 1924 on the Rossington Miners' Welfare Scheme. The architect for the scheme was Blythe Richardson of Doncaster and the builders were Wade & Boucher of Doncaster. These two postcard views were captured by James Simonton in the 1930s and feature the main building **(above)** and the gardens **(below)**. Bob Hughes, the Union representative, would often ride around the streets of New Rossington on his bicycle, ringing a hand bell to call the miners to union meetings at the welfare.*

Above: *An Aerofilm Series postcard of Rossington clearly showing the circular layout. The unknown writer has annotated the border of the card and written on the back as follows: "O O - Main Road, A - School, X - My Digs". The writer goes on to describe the area where they are lodging (in Grantham Street) "...this is Little Wigan – being mostly Lancs and rather an odd pack"!*

In 1928, there was an appeal to fund a new Doncaster Royal Infirmary hospital and the colliery company donated £4,000. The following year the village received its own ambulance station. The West Riding County Council later provided a clinic on McConnel Crescent. The first village libraries were housed in the Methodist Chapel on Nelson Road and in the wooden schools, but, in the late 1930s, Amalgamated Denaby Collieries donated a site for a permanent library on McConnell Crescent. Subsequently in 1940, West Riding County Council opened Rossington Library, built in an art deco style. In 1957 a Memorial Hall and health clinic were added next door.

Speaking at the Annual General Meeting of the Rossington Main Colliery Company Ltd, held on 29th March 1920 at the Royal Victoria Hotel in Sheffield, Lord Aberconway announced that the colliery company proposed to build a Miners' Institute and a 'cinema house' for the benefit of the workforce. On 5th June 1920, Frederick Hopkinson submitted plans on behalf of the colliery company for this cinema. However, building it was delayed and, on 18th November 1923, Frederick Hopkinson submitted revised plans. But again, these plans were unsuccessful and the plans for a colliery owned cinema were abandoned.

However, on 25th June 1925, the architects Blythe Richardson of Doncaster submitted plans for a cinema house on behalf of a private consortium. This too was delayed, and revised plans were submitted on 23rd January 1928. Finally, after the fourth attempt, Rossington received its cinema and the Rossington New Hippodrome was built at a cost of £15,000 on behalf of Mr J Williams and Mr H Minney of Chesterfield, the directors of the Clay Cross Hippodrome.

On Monday 1st July 1929, Rossington Hippodrome opened on Queen Mary's Avenue on a site next to the Royal Hotel. The building featured an auditorium with a capacity for 1,100 people, including 450 on the balcony. On opening night, a full house enjoyed a performance of *The Secluded Roadhouse*, a 1926 drama starring William Barrymore and Carol Vines. The building also included 8 dressing rooms behind the stage and thus was able to stage variety shows.

Above: *During its opening period, the Rossington Excelsior Brass Band was engaged to play concerts every day at the Hippodrome. The cinema passed into the ownership of S & E Cinemas (Chesterfield) Ltd and, despite a diversification into bingo, it was closed in 1962 and demolished shortly afterwards. A new shopping parade was built on the site.*

It was said that all your household requirements could be purchased from the shops of New Rossington. However, there was a need to serve the new community by public transport. From the railway station tickets could be booked through to Doncaster and even London but many villagers chose to catch buses direct from the village rather than walk to the railway station. Herbert Hancock operated a charabanc service to Doncaster but in 1919, there was speculation in the local newspaper in an article titled *"Scope for Great Enterprise, Dreams for the Future"* that Doncaster Corporation was looking to connect many of the surrounding mining villages with the town, and that they intended to extend their tramway from the Race Course all the way to Rossington. This plan did not come to fruition and at the end of 1922, Doncaster Corporation Transport commenced a motor bus service from the town to King's Avenue, terminating outside the Co-operative Stores. However, Doncaster Corporation were beaten to it by two independent bus operators, when in October 1920, George Ennifer - trading as Blue Ensign - started operating along the route, followed by John Barras – trading as Don Motors - who commenced a similar service in 1921.

Above: *A splendid view of King's Avenue in New Rossington looking south into The Circle, published by Edgar Scrivens in the mid-1920s. The motor bus is registered WT1933 and was a 30-seater Leyland vehicle delivered new in February 1924 to John Barras who traded as Don Motors. The vehicle was painted red and cream and was nicknamed 'the Red Don' by the people of the village. Don Motors commenced operating a bus service from Doncaster to New Rossington in 1921 and their buses were stabled overnight in the proprietor's garden behind his house on Bawtry Road, Bessacarr. In 1932 the above vehicle was sold for further service with Blackburn Corporation Transport. In 1962, John Barras retired and sold Don Motors to East Midland Motor Services who continued to operate a bus from Doncaster to Rossington until 1985. The smartly presented premises of the Doncaster Mutual & Industrial Co-operative Society on the left were built in 1915, the same year that the four shops on the right were completed.*

In 1923, the three operators along the route from Rossington to Doncaster were joined by a local man when William Morpus - trading as Rossie Motors - started a bus service. William Morpus was a Derbyshire man who had come to Rossington with the opening of the pit where he worked as a deputy. Morpus originally garaged his vehicles at Rossington Grange Farm but on 12th November 1927 he applied for permission to build a motor bus shed behind his new house, Coxley House, near Rossington Railway Station.

The four operators decided to combine their hourly services, providing a bus every 15 minutes from Doncaster to New Rossington and each operator was permitted to duplicate his trips at busy times. In 1962, Don Motors sold out to East Midland Motor Services and in 1974 Doncaster Corporation Transport merged with their counterparts at Sheffield and Rotherham to form South Yorkshire Passenger Transport Executive (SYPTE). The new combine pursued a policy of purchasing all the independent bus operators in the county and Blue Ensign was acquired in 1978 followed by Rossie Motors in 1980. In the mid-1980s, SYPTE-became sole operartors of the Rossington service when they exchanged route mileage elsewhere in the county with East Midland Motor Services. With deregulation in 1986 and subsequent privatisation, SYPTE was renamed South Yorkshire Transport, then Mainline, finally being purchased by First Bus in 1998.

Above: *A Doncaster Corporation Transport motor bus (fleet number 12, registration WY2835) seen outside the Co-operative Stores. The vehicle is a Bristol 4-ton bus with a capacity for 30 passengers and is seen here when newly delivered in 1924. The vehicle received a West Riding (WY) registration suffix, because the suffix DT wasn't allocated to Doncaster until 1927.*

Above and Below: *Although the 1930s were blighted by the economic depression and hardship that affected the industrial areas of the country, it wasn't all doom and gloom as demonstrated by the Rossington villagers shown enjoying the 1932 May Day Parade. This travelled the streets of New Rossington, and these two postcards were possibly pictured on Central Drive. Sadly, the identity of the participants is unknown.*

War-time 1939 —

We were evacuated to Rossington Sept. 1st. 1939 were billeted at the Royal Hotel (7 of us). Boys (6 or so) there are 2 Jws. Edith myself. Not a bad looking house is it. The 4 long windows downstairs used to be the restaurant, but now has been turned into a posh lounge. Bay window, is the smoke room & beyond that the Common tap room. You enter the middle door-way & the concert room stretches towards the back part of the house. The far door-way (where the dog is lying) is now the entrance for the A.R.P. & they use the rooms immediately above it. Our bedroom is over the 2nd. doorway, & the 3 windows over the 'bay' is our dining room. The other windows belong to rooms used by Mr & Mrs. Rhodes. That bit of building, nearly out of the picture, is the end of the picture house.

Above: *An interesting message on the back of a postcard of the Royal Hotel written during the Second World war by an unknown evacuee to Rossington.*

Post War Developments

Following the end of the Second World War, the need for the colliery to build up production was paramount and Doncaster Rural District Council decided to implement a house building programme. Thirty prefabricated bungalows were positioned behind the Station Hotel and 41 similar prefabs were built to form the Bank Wood Estate near the pit gates. However, these were only intended as a temporary fix for the housing problems and in the late 1940s the local authority completed the Grangefield Estate with an additional 36 houses and bungalows. Bevan Avenue is named after Aneurin Bevan, the Minster of Health with remit for housing. The prefabs at Bank Wood were demolished in 1965 and those on Bevan Avenue were cleared in 1979.

Above: *James Simonton recorded this view of the Airey Houses on Attlee Avenue in the mid-1950s. In the aftermath of the Second World War, under a dire need to address the country's housing shortages, W Airey & Sons Ltd created the Airey house, a factory-made house that could be quickly assembled from concrete slabs. The Airey houses at Rossington, like many of the other 20,000 examples built in the country were later reskinned in brick.*

In the late 1940s and 1950s, Attlee Avenue - with its concrete road surface typical of the time - was laid out, complete with 10 bungalows for retired miners, 46 council houses and 22 Airey Houses. The street is named after Clement Attlee who became Prime Minister in 1945 following the Labour Party's successful campaign in the General election.

In the early 1950s, the need to drastically address the national shortage of houses in industrial areas was met at Rossington by the National Coal Board and Doncaster Rural District Council. For many years Clay Flat Lane had been an old farm track connecting the second circle estate with Stripe Road, a route not suitable for motorised traffic. For many years the only access to New Rossington was by the level crossing over the busy railway line, and the barriers caused frequent delays. It is hard to believe now, but for the first 40 years of its life, the colliery village was once totally isolated from the surrounding towns and villages. The only way in and out for vehicular traffic was over the level crossing.

However, in the early 1950s, Clay Flat Lane was made into a road and the area to the north was a purchased by Doncaster Rural District Council for a new housing estate. This development consisted of 350 houses. Most of the streets in this estate were named after famous Labour Party politicians: Margaret Bondfield, Sir Stafford Cripps, James Keir Hardie, George Lansbury, Herbert Morrison, Lord Passfield (Sydney Webb), Robert Smillie & Ellen Wilkinson – the later giving her name to a new shopping parade in the development.

To the south of Clay Flat Lane, the Coal Industry Housing Association undertook another building project. This organisation was formed to develop and manage housing for the National Coal Board and to encourage miners from Scotland and the North East to move to new NCB estates constructed in the manpower deficient regions of Yorkshire and the East Midlands. All these estates feature similar houses constructed from grey or white concrete panels and at Rossington, 352 houses were laid out forming Beech Grove, Chestnut Avenue, Cherry Grove, Elmfield Road, Hazel Grove, Lime Tree Avenue and Oakdene.

During the 1950s, improvements continued to be made to the services and amenities of the area, necessitated by the village's increasing population - in 1951, this now numbered 10,190. Unlike many of the other pit villages surrounding Doncaster, the houses at Rossington had never been linked to an electricity supply from the colliery, and it wasn't until 1952 that electricity was laid on to the houses in the village. The water supply was also improved in 1954 when the original metal water tanks were replaced with a large purpose-built concrete water tower installed by the Tickhill Joint Water Board. The following year, a new public house was opened on Grange Lane, named the White Rose. New schools were built to serve the growing population at Grange Lane in 1953 with Tornedale Primary School following two years later to serve the children of the council and pit estates either side of Clay Flat Lane.

Above: *Grange Lane Primary School was built by the West Riding County Council to replace the old wooden huts schools. The new school was opened on 18th September 1952 by Alderman Robert Edwin Hughes, a notable figure amongst the local community. Mr Hughes started work at a small pit in Wales and at the age of 25 he moved to work at Rossington Colliery. He became the chairman of the local union committee and worked as check weighman. For 21 years he was also chairman of Rossington Parish Council and served Doncaster Rural District Council for 28 years as well as serving on the West Riding County Council where he was appointed alderman. The illustration above was recorded by James Simonton shortly after the school opened.*

In the late 1950s, Doncaster Rural District Council constructed a further 160 houses to the east of Gattison Lane and laid out Mayfield Crescent, Hunster Grove and Hesley Road.

The post-war building programme during the late 1940s and 1950s added an additional 976 houses in New Rossington plus 71 prefabricated bungalows, yet the NCB still required further housing. This was addressed in the 1960s when plans were drawn up for a large new housing estate constructed by Doncaster Rural District Council with grants from the NCB. This was the Radburn Road estate, so called because the houses were built on the Radburn Principle, a housing scheme first implemented in the town of Radburn, New Jersey, USA in 1929. Radburn housing features the backyards of houses facing a service street with the fronts of the properties facing each other over communal grassy areas.

From Grange Lane, a spine road named Radburn Road was constructed around the southern part of the second circle estate to link up with Gattison Lane and

Clay Flat Lane. Off the spine road, numerous cul-de-sacs were constructed (and named after winners of the Doncaster St Leger) along which the Radburn housing was built in blocks of 2, 4 and 6. Construction commenced at the western end in 1962 with 372 houses forming Phase 1 and this area is known as the 'Wimpey Estate' after the name of the builders, George Wimpey. The houses were built using a continually poured concrete method known as 'Wimpey-no-fines' referring to the type of concrete used – fine with no aggregates. A second smaller Radburn Principle scheme was built in the late 1960s when 70 houses were constructed adjacent to West End Lane on the site of the Bank Wood prefabs.

The original Radburn development was extended in the 1970s with an additional 220 houses and bungalows forming Phases 2 & 3; this time the properties were brick built. These houses were constructed by the building firm of Frank Haslam Milan on behalf of the local authority. Although, the Radburn development was constructed by the council, and the houses were available to all, the grant from the NCB stated that priority should be given to miners transferring from other coalfields, and many families from the North-East moved to this area, even establishing their own social club named the Radburn Club. At at the eastern end a new public house named The Poacher was built.

Other developments in the 1960s saw the construction of the Rossington Labour Club on Gattison Lane and a small supermarket opened on a plot of land across the road. On an adjacent site, the new Assembly of God Church opened in 1960, with the church built by the members of its congregation, replacing its former premises in an old tin hut on West End Lane. In 1966, on a site adjacent to the Miners' Welfare, a new indoor swimming pool was opened by Doncaster Rural District Council. One thing of concern to the local authorities was the lack of employment opportunities for women and this was met by the development of two clothes manufacturing plants built on West End Lane.

The 1970s also saw the construction of the first estates by private builders, along Bond Street in New Rossington and particularly in extensive developments in Old Rossington, a trend that has continued to the present day. Rossington was by now becoming increasingly attractive as a place of residence for those that worked in Doncaster and further afield, and this trend was coupled with a decline in the dominance of mining in the local population. Nevertheless, the facilities within the community continued to grow with Rossington Comprehensive School opening in 1969, followed by St Joseph's Roman Catholic School in 1976 and a Fire Station and Dental Clinic on West End Lane. The National Coal Board, always a somewhat reluctant landlord, had inherited around 1,570 pit houses from Rossington Main Colliery and went on to build another 352 to the south of Clay Flat Lane. At the end of the 1970s, the NCB were looking to dispose of their property portfolio, and all the former colliery houses in the village passed into the ownership of Doncaster Metropolitan Borough Council, although many were subsequently bought by private landlords and individsual tenants under the government's 'right-to-buy' policy.

Private building has continued into recent times, particularly in Old Rossington, and, in the 2011 census, the combined population of Old and New Rossington numbered 13,537. Since the closure of the pit in 2006, the local community has had to look outside for employment opportunities, and these have been partially met in recent times. In 2005, Doncaster-Sheffield (Robin Hood) Airport opened on the site of RAF Finningley and the development has since been linked by a new road known as the Great Yorkshire Way to the M18 motorway to the north of Rossington which opened in 2016.

A spur road has been built across the colliery site to improve transport links and Harworth Group PLC (the property development arm of UK Coal PLC), has been promoting the development of Pheasant Hill Park, a new town of 1,200 houses, complete with a supermarket, school and community buildings on the colliery site.

Today, the circular layout at the centre of New Rossington stands as a unique tribute to what was once built in the pursuit of coal. However, since the closure of the colliery, there has been plenty of ongoing development, and Rossington's claim to be the biggest village in England continues to be reinforced.

Glossary

Barnsley Seam. A highly prized seam of coal up to 10 feet thick within the Coal Measures of South Yorkshire. The coal seam is found at the surface near the town of Barnsley but lies buried at depth in the Doncaster area.
Bunker. A large container used for the storage of coal before it can be treated in the screens and washery of a coal preparation plant.
Cage. A steel structure used to transport men or coal filled tubs up and down the shafts. Some cages had two decks. The cage was attached by a steel rope to the winding engine.
Coal Measures. A thick sequence of rocks and strata which consists of sandstones, shales, clays and coal seams. The Coal Measures of Yorkshire contain around 30 different coal seams.
Coal Preparation Plant. A building where the treatment of coal is undertaken prior to dispatch, usually containing screens, washery and a conveyor leading to a rapid loading bunker.
Coalfield (Exposed & Concealed). An area of land above coal measure rocks. A coalfield may be "exposed", i.e. the coal measures are found at the surface, or "concealed" where they are hidden at greater depths beneath younger rocks. Doncaster is situated on a concealed coalfield where the coal measures are buried beneath Magnesian Limestone and Bunter Sandstones.
Drift. A sloping tunnel connecting coal seams to the base of the shafts or to the surface.
Fault. A geological fracture resulting from the upward or downward movement of rock strata.
Gob. The area left following removal of a coal seam. It is supported with waste material or allowed to collapse in a controlled way.
Headgear. A structure of wooden or steel lattice or reinforced concrete construction situated above the shafts and used to support the winding wheels.
Heapstead. A structure located beneath the headgear providing a covered means of transport for coal exiting the shafts via filled tubs enabling transport to the nearby screens buildings.
Longwall Mining. A method of coal working in which coal is mined from a long coal face. The coal face connects two tunnels which lead back to the base of the shafts. The coalface thus advances away from the shafts leaving an area of gob behind. This method was later replaced by retreat mining.
Main. A suffix used mainly in South Yorkshire to denote those collieries which mined the largest or main seam from the coal measures, i.e. the Barnsley Seam
Pit. A local term for a coal mine or colliery
Rapid Loading Bunker. A large bunker containing many tons of coal which are dropped into railway wagons passing beneath the structure.
Retreat Mining. The most economical method in mining in which roadways are driven out to the extremity of the royalty so that a coal face can then be worked back towards the shaft bottom. Largely superseded longwall mining in the 1950s/1960s.
Rake. A group of railway coaches or wagons all coupled together.
Roadways. Underground tunnels leading from the bottom of the shaft to the coal faces.
Royalty. An area of land beneath which coal can be extracted by paying a fee or royalty to the landowner on every ton produced.
Screens. A building containing numerous devices for sorting individual lumps of coal by size or weight.
Shafts. A vertical tunnel from the surface to the coal seam through which the coal is raised and men and materials can access the workings. Following a mining disaster at Hartley Colliery in County Durham each colliery was required to have two shafts, downcast and upcast, to aid escape in the event of an accident. Air was pumped through the downcast shaft to ventilate the workings and then drawn out of the colliery via the upcast shaft.
Shaft Pillar. An area of coal left intact in order to support the colliery's surface buildings and thus protect them from the effects of subsidence. Some coal was removed from the shaft pillar to form roadways or tunnels to access the underground workings.
Sinking. The process of tunnelling vertically downwards from the surface to the coal seam in order to construct a shaft, usually undertaken by workers called sinkers who specialised in this highly skilled but dangerous work.
Skip Winding. A method of winding coal up a shaft using a large capacity metal container or skip. A more economical way of transport than that previously used when individual coal filled tubs were brought to the surface in a cage.
Staithes. A landing stage for the loading of cargo into boats.

Tubbing. A waterproof casing, usually of iron, inserted into a shaft as it was sunk in order to keep back water and soft sediments.
Tubs. Small wagons used to transport coal underground, usually hauled by pit ponies.
Washery. A surface building for dealing with the cleaning and washing of coal.
Wayleave. A royalty paid to the owner of the land on which the colliery is situated.
Winding Engine. An engine, initially steam driven but later powered by electricity, used to raise the cages up and down the colliery shafts.

Further Reading

Abercrombie, P. and Johnson, T. H. (1922). **The Doncaster Regional Planning Scheme**, Hodder & Stoughton.
Adam, J. (2008) **A History of Rossington.** Rossington History Group.
Adam, J. (2012) **Rossington 1912-2012, a community built on coal.** Rossington History Group
Barnett, A L (1984) **The Railways of the South Yorkshire Coalfield from 1880.** RCTS Publishing.
Bulman, H F. (1920). **Coal Mining and the Coal Miner.** Methuen & Co Ltd.
Clarke, F A. (1986) **Rossington - glimpses into the past.** The Parochial Church Council of St Michael's Church, Rossington.
Clarke, F A. (1990) **Rossington - more glimpses into the past.** The Parochial Church Council of St Michael's Church, Rossington.
Colliery Guardian (1927) **The Colliery Year Book & Coal Trades Directory.** Louis Cassier Publishing.
Downes, E (2016) **Yorkshire Collieries 1947-1994.** Think Pit Publications.
Elliott, B. (2009). **South Yorkshire Mining Disasters Vol II: The Twentieth Century.** Wharncliffe Publishing.
Elliott, B. J. (2002). **The South Yorkshire Joint Railway & The Coalfield.** The Oakwood Press.
Edwards, D G (2001) **Historical Gazetteer & Bibliography of By-product Coking Plants in the United Kingdom,** Merton Priory Press.
Finney, M. (1995). **Men of Iron. A History of The Sheepbridge Company.** Bannister Publications.
Fordham, D (2015) **Maltby Main Colliery,** Fedj-el-Adoum Publishing.
Fordham, D (2017) **Dearne Valley Collieries, Communities & Transport.** Fedj-el-Adoum Publishing.
Grudgings, S (2015) **The last years of coal mining in Yorkshire.** Folly Books.
Hay, H & Fordham, D (2017) **New Coalfields New Housing: Reviewing the Achievements of The Industrial Housing Association.** Fedj-el-Adoum Publishing.
Hill, A. (2001). **The South Yorkshire Coalfield, a history and development.** Tempus Publishing, Stroud.
Jones, M (2017) **South Yorkshire Mining Villages.** Wharncliffe Books.
Kelly (1912) **Kelly's Directory of the West Riding of Yorkshire.** Kelly's Directories Ltd.
Leveridge, C & Fordham, D (2018) **The Yorkshire Coalfield, Pits and Mining communities depicted on a selection of old postcards and ephemera.** Fedj-el-Adoum Publishing.
Walters, Sir J Tudor (1927). **The Building of Twelve Thousand Houses.** Ernest Benn Publishing, London.
Williams, P (2005) **Images of Yorkshire Coal.** Landmark Publishing Ltd.
Yorkshire Amalgamated Collieries Ltd (no date c1928) **Modern Methods of Coal Production and Shipment.**